PARENTING

10 Basics of Conscious Childraising

PARENTING

10 Basics of Conscious Childraising

KARUNA FEDORSCHAK

BARNES & NOBLE BOOKS

NEW YORK

For support and inspiration,
special thanks to my husband and children,
and to my thorough editor, Regina

Published by MJF Books
Fine Communications
322 Eighth Avenue
New York, NY 10001

Parenting: 10 Basics of Conscious Childraising
LOC Control Number 2004104111
ISBN 1-56731-648-4

Formerly published as *Parenting: A Sacred Task*.
This edition published by arrangement with Hohm
Press.

Manufactured in the United States of America on
acid-free paper

MJF Books and the MJF colophon are trademarks
of Fine Creative Media, Inc.

QM   10   9   8   7   6   5   4   3   2   1

for
the Dazzling One

and
in loving memory of
C. Martin

CONTENTS

INTRODUCTION

*It is enough for a parent to keep a roof over
your head and food on the table, and to get
you up and off to school. Providing a cave of
security, a place for regressions is no small job.*
— James Hillman

I was a grown woman and mother before I made my
first pancake. My two young children had requested them
one weekend morning. We had been reading a book about
a boy who wants a pancake for breakfast. His mother, who
is busy working, directs her son to gather the ingredients
himself. And so, he collects eggs from the hen, he milks the
cow, and he takes grain to the miller to be ground into flour.
In our case, we found the necessary ingredients for our
"pancakes from scratch" in the pantry and refrigerator in
our kitchen. After measuring, mixing and cooking, I proud-
ly delivered several golden brown pancakes to the table. The
children ate in silence until I joined them and began to eat
my own. I was perplexed and disappointed to find that the
pancakes were doughy and heavy in the middle. Looking up

I saw the children had put down their forks. "Mom, we can't eat these," they said. "They're too gooey."

By the next time I tried my hand at pancakes I learned that a key ingredient had been missing from my first recipe. With the magical addition of baking soda, I made golden brown pancakes that were fluffy and light.

Parenting, like cooking, is an art. There was nothing like the hands-on experience of making those gooey pancakes to impress upon me the importance of baking soda. Similarly, there is nothing like raising children to make us aware of the missing ingredients in our character. Before I became a mother I felt successful at nearly everything I did. It seemed to me that I had a fairly sunny outlook on life and few bad days. As a mother I had my first real contact with the underbelly of my personality. I was frightened of the huge responsibility of caring for my first baby, resentful of the confinement and demands of mothering and often unsettled and on-edge, feeling that I had missed the training session for the job.

My first child was an active, inquisitive little person who seemed to thrive on projects and activities that required my alert attention and presence. I loved him dearly, but it was exhausting. Perhaps my biggest stumbling block was the misconception that parenting ought to be easy and if it wasn't, something was wrong. I was surprised to find my baby unpredictable and alive in a way that shattered my illusory sense of control and disrupted my well-ordered life.

Several years into this struggle, I learned I was pregnant with our second child. Since I already felt like a failure with my first, I couldn't imagine that another child would do anything but compound the situation. And in a way, that is exactly what happened. My parental load doubled. But my daughter turned out to be quite a different person than my son. Her arrival into our family unit was the exact ingredient needed – her presence provided balance and the opportunity to heal my relationship to my older child. When I was able to embrace my son's presence with gratitude and not retreat from the strong feelings that regularly got aroused in me, parenting became smoother and more fun, although not necessarily any "easier." The training program given by my son and daughter together (and it's not over yet!) has schooled me not only in the basics of mothering, but also in the foundations of human maturity.

There aren't too many of us who manage to ace the job of raising our children. A well-developed sense of humor is indispensable for the job. Indeed if we haven't got a sense of humor, we'll be given ample opportunity to work on it, because parenting can thrust us into unique situations such as we could never have imagined finding ourselves. A mother I know describes a very difficult transcontinental flight with her three young children where all three became airsick. They were throwing up in unison and in three different directions – onto her and surrounding passengers. In hindsight the story made us laugh so hard we had tears in our eyes, but at the time, that mother had some difficulty seeing the obvious humor in her situation.

There are few goals more worthy of our effort than to parent our children well. Parenting provides us a combination of necessity and opportunity. Once we invite a child into our lives, no matter what we think of the job, we will need to see the task through to completion. There is a real urgency to get it right when we realize we're in the process of molding a new life. At the same time, we are afforded the opportunity of a lifetime (theirs *and* ours) to parent our child well and to reap the benefits of what we learn in the process.

What constitutes a good parent really isn't all that mysterious. The aim of the wise parent is none other than to be in right relationship to his or her child. This simple yet radical goal presumes we are in some semblance of right relationship to ourselves to begin with. Since that is often *not* the case, we may be required to backtrack and set our own affairs in order while we work to meet the daily demand to show up for our child. To do that backtracking work we will likely need some assistance – perhaps in the form of a parenting book we read or the daily meditation we practice. We may turn to psychotherapy to bring some clarity to the unconscious motives that drive us. Maybe we will seek the honest feedback of a loved one, or take to heart the passing remark of a relative stranger.

When my first child was an infant and my need for help was at an all time high, I feverishly studied a half-dozen books on parenting. Although I got something out of each of them, it also became evident that I was *not* going to find my answers in someone else's book. During the course of my mothering, I also underwent psychotherapy and joined a mother's support group. As with my reading, these sources of help didn't have the specific answers to my questions. But more importantly, they taught me self-acceptance and provided fuel for my intention to do the job of mothering with as much love and integrity as I could. My determination to become a skillful mother, catalyzed by the daily experience of raising two young children, was the recipe for getting it right with me so I could get it right with my kids.

CONSCIOUS PARENTING

What is conscious parenting and what does this book have to say that is any different from what's already been said? Conscious parenting assumes the perspective that having children and parenting is spiritual practice, as much a path as sitting meditation or *koan* work. *
Parenting-as-practice, like any genuine spiritual practice, has the intention to grow the soul and purify the character of the parent. In this way the conscious parent becomes qualified to care for the soul of the child. Such a parent is willing to examine their habits, beliefs and training, even their biological impulses; and intends to act against these habits or impulses, if necessary, for the greater good of their growing child.

An older women friend who raised her children through two failed marriages, confided to me that, at the time, she was blind to the fact that the home environment her kids grew up in would shape the adults they were to become. Their difficult childhood experiences led each of them to significant crises in adulthood. This mother's remorse cannot change the past, but she has earned genuine life wisdom and compassion through her mistakes. Today she is a caring and important presence in the lives of her grandchildren.

---

* Koan work refers to the Zen spiritual practice whereby the abbot or roshi gives the student a verbal puzzle to solve during meditation. In order to find the answer to the koan, the practitioner must make a radical shift in understanding from his ordinary limited perspective to one of a broader reality.

Everybody learns something from parenting, if only in hindsight. How can we not? But whether we have a child by surprise, or after much prayer and anticipation, we are going to find ourselves at the effect of our parenting "program" (that's the one we had modeled for us). The conscious parent intends to serve their child's objective best interest, and in the process, to honestly face their own shortcomings. To parent as a spiritual practice doesn't guarantee we'll be able to transcend this unconscious parenting program. In fact, a lot of what it may entail is clearly observing how much we are *not* beyond our conditioning. Although we may be tempted to willfully change what we do not like in ourselves, the conscious parent realizes that the only lasting solution is to practice ruthless self-observation and generous self-acceptance in order to nurture the possibility to be different than his or her unconscious program.

Although I had twelve years of traditional spiritual practice and relationship to a spiritual teacher under my belt when I became a mother, the changes to my lifestyle that came with childraising really knocked me for a loop. I did not have the familiar support of my formal practice. There was no space for it in my new life. True, I seized any opportunity to sit or study or exercise, and there *were* little windows of time, as my children grew, during which I could practice formally. But that was not to be counted on, and often when I did have a little time to myself I was too exhausted to do anything but sleep. It took me years to learn to make mothering itself a practice. Through the surrender of my formal practice to the necessity of caring for my children, I discovered both the real value of formal practice, and its genuine essence outside of any form. As my kids have grown, I have been able to reintegrate formal practice into my life as a mother. I find I can only be the kind of parent I aspire to be when I am also engaging daily meditation, exercise and study of spiritual teaching.

In writing the present volume, I have taken inspiration from the book *Conscious Parenting* (Hohm Press, 1997) by my spiritual teacher, Lee Lozowick. His formal teaching work places particular emphasis on preserving the innocence of children through wise parenting. In the foreword to *Conscious Parenting*, Purna Steinitz describes it as a "workbook." A workbook, Steinitz says, has the possibility to shift the reader into a whole new outlook.

When I first read *Conscious Parenting* I was hard hit by its decidedly critical, almost pessimistic, tone. It was as if to parent consciously was an unreachable goal. Lozowick is uncompromising in his assertion that a wise parent isn't made without the willingness and ability to struggle against unconsciousness. Upon further study of the book, however, I found beyond the criticality a really thorough and kind treatise on the basics, plus an underlying mood or tone that is a guide to the specifics of parenting. Tuning into the appropriate mood from which conscious parenting derives will fill us in on the specifics as if they were written in invisible ink between the lines on the page. That's why *Conscious Parenting* is a workbook. Aligning with the author's understanding, we fall into that mood. We then naturally know things about parenting we didn't think we knew. That kind of experience can happen with one reading, but will only become established in us by working more consistently with the material, using the book as a *workbook*. Perhaps the only value any book on parenting really has to offer is the author's context. In the present volume, too, I believe my orientation or context– the mood of this book – has more potential value than the particulars the reader will find here.

Mood and Form

Parenting: 10 Basics of Conscious Childrasing is divided into ten chapters, each exploring one of the ten basics of conscious parenting. Two key aspects underlie each of the ten – each basic has a *mood* or feeling, and each has a *form* or appearance. Unless mood and form are married, the expression of each basic will be incomplete. For example, my own children are so utterly attuned to any mood of irritation or impatience from me, that no matter how right my words (the form) may be, what they get is the mood (in this case, negative) from which I am speaking.

Conversely, it is possible *to get to* mood through form. In other words, if I do the right thing or "act as if," there can be a rather miraculous shift of my mood into proper alignment with my words or intentions. I can invoke genuine mood. I have at times had the presence of mind to do this, by not allowing my speech (the form) to give away my bad mood, and have gotten a positive response from my children.

The ideal is to have our actions come from the right internal mood or context. This will not always be the case because we are humans, whose ability to parent consciously is a work in progress. Therefore it is valuable to be able to do the right thing even on a tough day. Generally though, the appropriate mood will give rise to the necessary form. In other words when we are resting in a mood of love and acceptance toward our children, we will generally know what to do in response to their needs in any given moment. When the proper mood and form come together in our parenting practice, then the ten basics appear as needed.

And how do we get to the appropriate mood and form for any given situation? It can happen spontaneously from time to time and will then serve as a reminder and a reference point for the future. Out of nowhere I will sometimes do exactly the right thing with one of my kids, like holding firm on a boundary with the perfect mixture of strength and softness, and think, "Wow that was great! Did I do that?"

We may see someone else manifest the right mood/ form with our child (or another child), and in that way make a connection. I have gotten some big clues on how to improve my parenting from observing my children's school teachers interact with my own children and others. But the day to day work toward appropriate mood and form is through *education* (that is experience, observation, study), *intention* (the deep desire to get beyond our limitations to serve our child), *help* (support and feedback from friends and/or professionals), *prayer* (supplication to the higher power to guide us), and a little *magic* (the impossible possibility).

Re-Mapping the Way

Children bring out both the best and the worst in us. As parents we find our strongest qualities highlighted, and our weakest points on full display. It is widely acknowledged in the experience of many parents that the first child in particular seems to provoke the full barrage of our unconscious, unresolved issues as adults. As they move through the various stages of their growing up, our children bring to the surface whatever we didn't work out in our own upbringing, whatever wounding we carry from our family of origin. It's a lawful and predictable process whereby each developmental stage of our child, especially the *first* child, invokes our own experience of the same stage when *we* were small. Understandably, our ability to parent our child through the various steps of his or her growing up is affected by the overlay of our own experience as a child with each of the same steps.

Amazingly, the adult psyche contains a perfectly detailed map of what happened in childhood. We live at the effect of that map every day of our lives, generally unconscious of its power over us. We rely upon this map to navigate our world. At times we may sense that the details of the map are not entirely correct or useful when we run into snags in our close relationships or on the job. The confusion and intensity of feelings that arise on those occasions signal us that we are on a section of the map that is incomplete or inaccurate. There's nothing like being a parent to experience a full-on encounter with our mismapping.

While it's unlikely that anyone can be a parent and remain untouched by the job, it's also unlikely that real change will occur for us without the right mix of intention and the basics presented here. There's no escaping the heartbreak of seeing our children at the effect of the aggression and ignorance that characterize our modern world. From birth on, they will encounter it in people and in the environment around them. The only useful response is to be willing to work on *our own* unconsciousness, because we are our child's first contact and experience of the world.

In order to be a wise parent, we must refocus the purpose of our lives from the accumulation of achievements and possessions, to the building of the presence and wisdom required to nurture a new life. When we've recovered from the shock of realizing our relative poverty in these domains, we may naturally begin to question what the genuine roles of mother and father are.

Mother and Father

As expectant parents awaiting the birth of our first child, we have for the first time the necessity and motivation to discover our genuine possibility as mature men and women in the roles of mother and father. The awakening of our potential as mother or father is part of the larger picture of learning to parent with wisdom. The template or archetype for mother and father contain the keys to our highest possibility as parents, and the necessary wisdom to not only guide a child's growth to adulthood, but also to pattern him or her to become a conscious parent in turn.

Although this is a parenting book for both mothers and fathers, it is my assumption that women are naturally responsible for the lion's share of the sacred task of childraising, especially in the early years. After all, a child is conceived and grown within a woman's body and is birthed from her. For most of the first year or more of an infant's life, a mother is (ideally) engaged in breastfeeding her infant. That creates a powerful organic connection between mother and child. Moreover, fathers are still generally the breadwinners, even in modern families. A man's job or work typically takes him outside the home, which obviously limits the amount of time a father spends with his kids.

That leaves mothers with the bulk of the task of raising children. Although this is not necessarily a dismal scenario, it certainly can be. It takes a resourceful woman to mother young children all day long and stay emotionally intact herself. But this *is* a mother's work. For all our hopes to be liberated, and beyond sexual stereotyping in our parenting roles, it's not really a man's job to change diapers and wipe noses. Men are not instinctively maternal in this way. That's not to say a father would never participate in the mundane care of his children, only that it is not primarily his work to do so. A father's focus is on providing for his family. When a father spends time with his children, he may be more naturally inclined to wrestle with them or teach them, than he is to fix them dinner. Some families have reversed these traditional roles and have not only made it work but found it to be really beneficial to all concerned. I would call these situations the exception to the rule.

When our kids were young my husband periodically, and seriously, offered to exchange jobs with me. Although I struggled mightily at times with the daily task of mothering, I never wanted to take him up on his offer. I knew that children need mothers. In my effort to mother consciously and lovingly, I bumped up against myself at times in very unpleasant ways, thus prompting my husband to so generously offer to relieve me of my burden. But I knew that this bumping was an important process that had life-changing possibility for me and for my children, if I could persevere with it in the right way. I wasn't going to just bail out in the middle of a project of this magnitude! I knew that I could make this mothering work my practice and my joy, and I was determined to stick with it until it was. Through that perseverance I have uncovered some of the wisdom and resourcefulness of the archetypal woman and mother that lay dormant within me until I really needed to find it.

Many mothers are single or working or both. If a woman is parenting without a partner, then in some ways she will need to be both mother *and* father to her children. If she is working, she will need to insure the best of care for her children in her absence, and the continuity of her emotional connection to her children and theirs to her. If she is both single and working outside the home, her job is truly a challenging one. Even given obstacles of this magnitude, I still believe it is possible to be a conscious and content parent to our children, because conscious parenting is a disposition, not a prescribed set of conditions.

No special course of study is required to realize our gender roles as parents, because our knowing of them is innate to us as men and women. Given the proper conditions, genuine motherly-ness or fatherly-ness will naturally flower. What we do need is a *culture* of men and women in which to rest. A woman needs to spend time with other women, and a man with other men. When a man and a woman focus on only one another for support and self-reflection as a couple *and* as parents, they miss the crucial perspective provided by other parents of the same sex.

While none of the ten basics that follow are *gender specific*, our uniquely masculine or feminine approach will color our expression of each. As we consider each of the basics in turn, a picture will (hopefully) emerge of mother and father as conscious parents. We can take those images as the seed of possibility. Our own parenting path will lead us to our particular feminine or masculine expression as a mother or father.

THE SACRED TASK

When we commit to parenting-as-practice, we step onto a labyrinthine path with no sure-fire guarantee that we will complete the course to become a conscious parent. From out of our confusion and need can be forged real understanding and acceptance, and genuine transformation. Real understanding of the job allows us to parent with wisdom. Acceptance means our honest acknowledgment of our human failure to meet the mark. Transformation encompasses the real possibility that we can change for the better.

While confusion and "not knowing" may characterize a large part of the journey, at regular intervals along the way we may (mercifully) find ourselves at a vantage point of genuine knowing and clarity. In those moments we can take a deep breath, drink in the view and give thanks for the needed perspective before plunging back into the thick undergrowth of the trail.

The "basics" described in this book – love, attention, boundaries, food, touch, help, humor, respect, relaxation, holding on and letting go – are all facets of the diamond of the mature parent. When we make parenting our practice, we magnetize these essential qualities to ourselves. By rubbing up against them over and over, in both triumph *and* defeat, they can eventually rub off on us.

PARENTING

10 Basics of Conscious Childraising

LOVE
The 1st Basic

Taking It

Children love us without reserve. That kind of love can be as hard to take as the discomfort, noise, and general confusion these active, inquisitive, growing little beings bring into our lives as well. Their unqualified love is as much in our faces as their innocent expectation that we will love them as fully in return.

The love of a child can be hard to receive when as adults we operate on the psychological belief that we are unlovable. A child is a twenty-four-hour-a-day broadcast that our belief is in error. And yet amazingly, tragically, we can enroll our children in the same belief in scarcity of love by persisting in it ourselves for long enough. Blessed indeed is the child who has a parent willing and able to surrender their "unlove" and relearn a new way of living in apprenticeship to their child. Blessed indeed is the child (and the parent) who has a "tribe" – a wise extended family or spiritual community – to hold and nurture them,

1

and whose various members can fill in the pieces that the parents are missing and are thus unable to provide for their child themselves.

Having a child or children in our lives is a call to do the joyous, backbreaking, heart-opening, painful job of becoming whole again, in the role of parent, in order to meet that child in his or her natural wholeness. "Taking" the love of our children means accepting that we are lovable. In order to do that we must give up our self-hatred and negativity. There is no formula, no hard and fast rule, and no easy "how-to" for the sacred task of parenting. Sometimes groping painfully along, other times soaring majestically, nonetheless we get up every morning and begin again whether today brings the groping, the soaring, or more likely both!

Giving It

Holding our newly born child in our arms it is all so simple. We have only to love this little being and nothing more or less is required. After those first moments, the picture tends to become less clear. When our baby is tiny, we may worry about nursing and weight-gain, colic and jaundice. A newborn is so incredibly vulnerable. Therein lies the wonder and the terror of parenting an infant. So it goes as they grow. Each stage brings new joys, new worries. And that simple truth that was so evident when we first laid eyes on them can become buried in the details of life. When our willful toddler throws his first temper tantrum, or our pre-teen mouths off at us, it is much more difficult to remember the bottom line: They want to know we love them. We are called upon to show up with the correct expression of that love in any given circumstance. When all else fails, and it's bound to, it never hurts to take them in our arms, if they'll let us, and *tell* them we love them. If we can do that, get to that place where it's possible to offer our love and for our child to receive it, it will be like we've pushed the reset button – a button that is likely to need pushing more than once. Being a parent is intensive, demanding work.

Several days after the birth of my first child, he began to show signs of jaundice. His skin and the whites of his eyes were yellowish. He was lethargic, sleeping a lot and not waking up to nurse. My husband and I took him to the lab for a blood test and discovered he would need to be hospitalized immediately.

For the next three days we camped out in the intensive care unit at the local hospital. I took the day shift with a loyal woman friend for support; my husband took the nights with my friend's husband for company. I was exhausted from the birth, overwhelmed with my new responsibility and fearful for my baby's health. I wandered back and forth between the family room attached to Intensive Care and the bathroom down the hall. My days and nights were punctuated with the dutiful periodic pumping of milk from my overfull breasts to insure I didn't lose the capacity to nurse. I was in a delirium of fatigue and anxiety, feeling as vulnerable as my newborn under the "bili lights" in his clear plastic crib in the ICU. I loved him so desperately that I couldn't bear to think about what I would do if I lost him.

On the third day my husband and I were notified that our son's liver was fully functioning and he was cleared to

3

leave the hospital with us. Relieved and elated, we returned home after this unexpected crisis to resume our new-baby routine of nursing and napping and loving this new little life that was now and forever bound up with ours. My husband and I had both had our eyes opened about just how real this could get, and all this in the space of one week from our baby's homebirth to his release from the hospital following jaundice. It was evident that our concepts about "giving" love had been redefined by our nearness to the mysteries of life and death. We had come light years in the blink of an eye. Yes, we were going to have to grow up; there was no doubt about it. And we couldn't have been given a better impetus to do so than this child. To grow our son outside the womb, we were going to have to nourish in ourselves the qualities of kindness, patience, courage, gratitude, and more – in short, all the facets of love.

Mother Love

A woman grows her child within her womb and usually assumes the greater share of the burden of raising the child. Mother is a child's first and most significant role model in life. The expectation of acceptance and love from mother is the blueprint every child is born with. Love and acceptance are either communicated or not in every single interaction a mother has with her child from birth on. While that might sound like an impossible standard, it is simply a statement of fact.

If this expectation has generally been honored, any breach of it will be met with loud and long protest from a child until the flow of love and acceptance is restored. Love and acceptance create a mood in which the child is subtly "cradled." Both inform a mother's every action – the way that she touches her child, the sound of her voice, her very breathing. The infant is entirely one with his mother and thus has no defense against anything he perceives that is *other than* love and acceptance.

Basic Goodness

It could be said that every troublesome behavior, every bad mood or act of meanness on the part of an older child can be traced back to the basic question, "Am I loved?" Every action of ours that does not communicate love and acceptance for our child casts doubt on the validity of the basic expectation with which he or she was born. That is not to say that every time a child misbehaves or protests our treatment of him or her, we have somehow breached their trust. Love is a context that is not bound by any particular form. But if a child receives love and acceptance in good measure, then he or she will have the foundations of a sense of "basic goodness." Basic goodness is a term used by the great contemporary Tibetan teacher Chögyam Trungpa Rinpoche. His book, *Shambhala: The Sacred Path of the Warrior* (Shambhala Publishers, 1984), elucidates this fundamental principle:

> It is not just an arbitrary idea that the world is good, but it is good because we can *experience* its goodness. We can experience our world as healthy and straightforward, direct and real, because our basic nature is to go along with the goodness of situations. The human potential for intelligence and dignity is attuned to experiencing the brilliance of the

5

bright blue sky, the freshness of green fields, and the beauty of the trees and mountains. We have an actual connection to reality that can wake us up and make us feel basically, fundamentally good. (p. 31)

A mother communicates her orientation to the world with her body and her actions while her infant is in-arms. Because a child experiences him or herself as one with the mother, *her* relationship to basic goodness is also the child's. The mother's actions of nursing her child when he or she is hungry, and keeping her child securely in-arms and close to her body establish this sense of basic goodness in the child. That child's needs are being met in accord with the "blueprint" with which he was born. The soft smile on an infant's lips as he finishes nursing and drifts off into contented sleep in his mother's arms says it all.

Welcoming a Child

A mother's job entails making her child feel welcome in this world. By her willing care of her infant a mother expresses this welcome in action. A child who feels welcome is likely to be more relaxed and content dealing with her new infant body and the wide world of new sights and (no longer muffled!) sounds that greet a child at birth. By contrast, a child who does not feel welcome or is receiving mixed signals from her world, may squirm and fuss without apparent cause and look generally unhappy. This is not to say that every fussy baby is uncomfortable because her mother is not welcoming her properly; that would be overly simplistic in the extreme. But even the most unsophisticated observer knows the difference in overall demeanor between a baby received wholeheartedly by her family and one who comes into a circumstance marked by mixed feelings and tension.

A new mother may feel nervous and insecure with her responsibility. That is perfectly natural. If she will simply rest in her underlying sense of connectedness and love for her child, her concerns will be eased and any information she is lacking will naturally come to her. Any mother with more than one child can generally testify to the difference between her first child and the children that follow. With a first child, mothers often feel an exaggerated sense of responsibility for even the child's natural development from one stage of life to the next, as if the child's first teeth would never appear if his mother didn't will it. Taking one's role that seriously makes a strong communication to the growing child who is at the effect of it. Studies show that birth order is a significant element in character formation. First children tend to be more high-strung, difficult, or fussy than children who come later in the birth order. That disposition can and does follow a child throughout life.

After her first child, a mother will tend to be less obsessive in monitoring the growth and development of subsequent children. Every little twitch or glitch along the way is no longer cause for alarm. As such, these children and their mothers are more relaxed. Experienced mothers learn to trust the biological blueprint in charge of the growth and development of the human species. Such mothers know that freedom from undue attention allows a child to grow and mature innocently and naturally.

Father Love

After mother, father is a child's most important bond and role model. A father serves his child in the transition from the arms of mother into the wider embrace of the world. When a child is held by his father, it is a different experience from a mother's embrace. Father's arms communicate love in the form of strength and detached compassion. He understands a child's vulnerability and innocence in a way unique from mother. Father is both the protector of his vulnerable young child, and an impartial proponent of his child's ability to grow out of that helplessness. A father teaches his child the first lesson in separation from mother. In receiving the child naturally and confidently from mother's arms, father makes a physical teaching about the all-rightness of letting go. Fathers also expect their children will fulfill their potential to show up in the world.

Being strong does not mean that father is some kind of he-man who lifts weights everyday. His strength may or may not have a physical component. Father's strength is his objective relationship to the world. The archetypal masculine context sees through the illusion of all appearances. As such father's very presence is a communication of that truth, which we could call objective love. Because he relates to the world in a more detached way, father has an inherent understanding of the nature and value of discipline. He offers that perspective to his children both by example and by direct instruction.

As the perfect complement to mother's unconditional love and acceptance, father's love encompasses the expectation that his kids will relate to work and discipline in age-appropriate ways. Traditionally a father would not only model hard work, but also teach his skills to one or more of his children. Our modern world is rather different in this regard, but I believe a father still has the potential to fulfill this model in some form within his family. While he may not teach his children a trade, a father is still rightfully the leader or head of his family, and can offer instruction or guidance in that role.

Modeling Love Together

In any family, conventional or not, the possibility is for father and mother to blend their unique perspectives to the benefit of all. When, as parents, we are tolerant of one another's foibles and appreciative of one another's strengths, then we are modeling love for our children.

For instance, I think my husband has his head in the clouds with regard to certain aspects of home and family, but honestly, he has the same criticism of me. We get irritated and annoyed with one another because we don't think about the same things. Yet that is exactly how it is supposed to be. We each pay attention to different aspects of home and family, but we don't tend to appreciate one another for that. When, to my perception, my husband's head is in the clouds, he might be, for instance, making plans for how we'll get the money to go on an especially ambitious family vacation and still cover the mortgage. When my head is in the clouds, I might be planning dinner or pondering my daughter's recent mood, asking the question, "What might she be needing?" When we show respect and regard for our partner, that's parenting as practice.

In truth we all unconsciously believe that how we are is the only right way to be. If we are to model love together, we must be able to see past that egocentric perspective. That is the interpersonal work we must all be capable of doing if we are to build love with *anyone*. We strive to practice kindness, generosity and compassion with one another because it's the right thing to do, and also because it makes life together ever so much more enjoyable. My work is to accept and love my husband for the man that he is, while not losing sight of the important work of blending our perspectives in our marriage and family life. That's the goal, and whether we achieve it perfectly or not, it counts that we're trying. Our children don't expect perfection, but they do benefit from our honest efforts to model love.

For a man or a woman, the qualities of fatherly or motherly love that have been described can be distorted by an unhealthy psychology. For instance, the man whose masculine strengths have been thwarted or discounted in his life experience offers the negative expression of strength and discipline. And likewise, a woman whose feminine qualities have been discounted or abused will have difficulty expressing motherly love in a healthy way. We are all mostly examples of wounded psychology and thus must work to build a connection to the objective essence of mother and father despite the obstacle of our less-than-optimal life experience. It is not only possible to do this, but actually the difficulty we each have to overcome contains the seed of our unique strength.

We might say that loving our children is the easy part. Feeling love for our children is natural. Love comes first in the list of basics in this book because it underpins the rest of the qualities presented here. The remaining basics arise in the presence of love. But just feeling love for our children is not enough. With the proper discipline and intention, love will produce wise action. Then we will have realized love that transcends mere sentiment.

ATTENTION
The 2nd Basic

Children need our attention. In the beginning we must pay attention to their cues and learn their signals for hunger, sleep, diaper changes, burping, touch and so on. Their bodily needs are immediate and organic. When toddlers first begin to walk, we must pay attention in order to guide them on a safe course through an often sharp-edged world. In the middle years of childhood the emotional need for attention comes to the fore and we find ourselves more tangibly responsible for nourishing both their bodies *and* their growing psyches. Our kids want to know that we see them for who they are and aspire to be. They want to be sure we love them and are willing to attend and support their emerging identity. Here the challenge is to anchor them without either deflating or inflating their young egos.

Throughout childhood, it's also important to pay attention to our child's relationship with siblings and playmates, particularly when they are clashing. It's our job to prevent them from hurting one another and to teach them how to constructively resolve their differences. If we are paying attention we will also notice when we need to give boundaries to a growing child. As they get older and our attention on them is less constant, it's especially important to notice the ways in which they need us to support, validate and guide them as they set a course for adulthood.

As parents, the skill of knowing how to prioritize the things that demand our attention is indispensable. If we are parenting as practice we will want to be able to respond to the highest need for our attention, and not just pay attention in the way we are most inclined. For instance, when my children were young we lived in a busy household with extended family where the phone was forever ringing. Although it wasn't always an easy practice, I chose to make my children's needs a priority over answering the telephone. It was evident to me that my attention was pretty well consumed with the care of my children, and equally clear that I rarely needed to take the incoming calls. They were often for someone else, or if the call was for me, it could nearly always wait.

It was also my intention that conversations with friends, whether in person or over the telephone, not exclude the child tugging on my sleeve. I don't agree that kids should be allowed to run roughshod over our lives, but we ought to give them the same respect we would give anyone who asks for our attention. It may be that we ask them to wait until we're done, or if our conversation isn't important enough to make them wait, we pause right away to see what they need.

The conscious parent is always asking himself where his attention is best placed at any given time. For me, developing the willingness and ability to drop what I am doing to respond to the needs of my children has been a challenge. I have become less concerned with what others think, and more focused on what I know to be right. I also learned to surrender my single-pointed focus on getting things done, in favor of the call for relationship and heart-fulness with my family.

Babies

After having two children of my own I was fortunate to share in the early childhood years of a friend's son. When Daniel had barely begun to toddle and was not yet speaking, I was startled to observe how clearly he communicated his wants and needs. Happily, his mother was as responsive as he was communicative. I watched one morning as with grunts and gestures he directed his mother to get him a bowl of oats with raisins and milk. Daniel's success with his mother no doubt encouraged his expressiveness, yet I believe every child is like this in his or her own way. From infancy on, if we care to notice, children broadcast their needs and wants loud and clear. Our job, indeed our delight, is to pick up the signal. That is not to say there aren't times, particularly in infancy, when we just do not know what our child needs. Is she hungry or sleepy? Does she have gas or need to burp or have her diaper changed? Is she responding to stress or tension in the environment, teething pain, or a growth spurt that is creating generalized discomfort? At these times we simply do our best to make our child comfortable. In general though, with attention and experience, we can enjoy a fairly easeful and clear channel of communication with our pre-verbal youngster.

Aside from keeping our baby physically close and feeding him when he's hungry, our attention naturally includes creating a bubble of safety around our new child. That means we carry our infant securely at all times (soft baby carriers and slings are great for this) so that he or she feels no fear of being dropped. We also guard our child against aggression from ourselves and others. Aggressive behavior toward a baby is any form of attention or activity that violates that baby's personal space or safety. Aside from monitoring our own hostile moods toward our child, we will also want to protect a baby against physical aggression from other children, particularly older siblings. We will want to be on the lookout as well for the unwelcome attentions of an adult who gets too close to the baby or uses language (generally unconsciously) that is disrespectful to the child.

In many traditional cultures, the early weeks of an infant's life are spent sheltered in the home, in-arms. Whether we observe such a period of seclusion or not, we will at least want to avoid chaotic public settings like discount department stores, busy street fairs, even large grocery stores until a baby's nervous system is mature enough to withstand the psychic barrage of these environments.

Toddlers

When the toddler years arrive we may fondly reflect back on infancy when, despite the lost sleep and the constraint of having a child constantly in-arms, the parenting experience is relatively idyllic. Although babies are fairly vocal about their needs, they are not willful in the way of the toddler. After the many months of more stationary, in-arms mothering, we are now called upon to move, and move quickly, in pursuit of the questing toddler. What is required at this stage is to stay with or contain our child to properly attend him.

By "contain" I don't mean in a playpen. Although there might be a time and place for this piece of baby equipment, I am skeptical of the value of playpens. Toddlers should *not* be allowed to trash the house or totally monopolize our time and attention, but given the choice between a playpen and a childproofed living room, I would go for adapting the environment rather than containing the child. A toddler's *modus operandi* is to move and explore. We can expect extreme frustration and/or temper tantrums if we routinely confine our toddler child for convenience, and I say we deserve what we get when we disrespect a child in this way.

The responsible parent is willing to pay attention. Yes it is difficult, demanding and disruptive of our ordinary routines. But this is what we signed on for when we asked for the blessing of a child in our well ordered lives. We can accommodate the toddler's need to explore – and preserve our own sanity – by thoroughly childproofing at least one space in our home, as well as by planning regular outings to the park or any other location where our child or children can range freely and safely within sight of us. At this stage it is not realistic, for instance, to expect our active toddler to sit still in the seat of a shopping cart while we do a full-scale food shop. We learn to be creative about handling such practicalities, and more understanding about our child's limited capacity to be confined. And life goes on. Before we know it, these years have passed and we may reminisce about them fondly as well.

The toddler years typically include bumps and bruises. The child of two, three and four is a determined adventurer who is undaunted by a little pain. Although she may protest loud and long an unexpected knock on the head, the toddler is usually off and running again before the tears have fully dried. And that is as it should be. Our job as attendant is to protect our child from life-threatening injury. If we are able to prevent minor bumps from happening, that is well and good. Beware the idea that we should try to protect our child from any physical pain. That is not possible or useful. The toddler learns from her painful encounters with the solid world around her. That is right and natural. But when bumps and bruises result from our lack of proper attention, that gives our child the message that she is not worthy of our care and attention – a message that goes in deep and lasts a lifetime.

Balance is needed. We can hone our awareness of when to fully attend and when to attend in a more diffuse way. Both qualities of attention are necessary and useful. Practicing one or the other exclusively will not work. Some parents tend to err on the side of using mostly diffuse attention. Their child *is* in their field of attention, but details go unnoticed. By the time this parent responds to her toddler's howl of pain or indignation, she is too late to see the full picture of what happened. Did he fall down? Did his playmate hit him with a toy? Other parents attempt to exert full-on focused attention at all times. This is exhausting for the parent and stifling for the child. Because this parent is following every detail up close, he may miss the ways in which even a young child can begin to act autonomously from his or her parent. This parent is over-involved in his child's activity.

My observation is that most parents are *inclined* to pay attention either diffusely or in sharp focus. The key is to be able to attend both ways as needed. To this end we may want to elicit the feedback of others to find out which kind of "attender" we are. Experience will teach us the value of both qualities of attention.

The School-Age Child

As a child approaches the school years, emotional and social life comes to the fore. For starters, a child who will attend nursery school, playgroup or kindergarten begins the process of separating from mother. Some sort of separation from mother at age four to five years or so is healthy and natural. The separation doesn't have to be dramatic, in fact it would be better if it were not. But taking a step toward independence from mother is emotionally timely for most children, not as a rule but a general guideline.

Some parents I know who are practicing "attachment-style" parenting (that means nursing, co-sleeping, "baby-wearing," etc.) are reticent to let go at this stage. It's important to take our child's cues as to readiness and trust our own intuitive sense of what is right, but also important to pay attention to the inclination to cling unnecessarily to our children. When my first child reached this age, I badly needed some time to myself yet I had come to view myself as indispensable to him. I honestly could not conceive how my son could manage without me. I was unconsciously giving him the message that it wasn't okay to take the next step away from me. When I saw what I was doing, I willed myself to take a risk and release him. What was holding me back from letting go was *my* fear, not that of my child. My tendency was to hold on and I had to learn to make adjustment for that.

Children are born with tendencies of *their own*. Not everything our child struggles with is the result of some failing on our part as a parent. But in order to help a child with their fears and insecurities, we ought to have some clarity about our own. If we do not, supporting our child through simple developmental steps such as we are considering here, can become a bigger challenge than it would otherwise be.

Assuming we are able and willing to release our children to fulfill their developmental blueprint at this stage of their lives, we also should look out for the tendency to let go of too much too soon. Sometimes we don't see what our child needs from us, or maybe we are tired of working so hard at paying attention and feel we deserve the break provided by playgroup or school to get away from our child. At times we *do* need a break from our kids and they from us. But if we take a break from our child in a way that she feels as a rejection, that is not useful. If we make a habit of rejecting our child (however that looks in our case) when we are overwhelmed with our parenting responsibilities, that rejection will eventually backfire on us – perhaps dramatically in the teen years. There are times when every parent feels like they would like to hand off the childraising job to someone else for a year or two. Usually that feeling passes. After a break, we are renewed and once again able to connect to the real joy that is possible in the company of children. So we do our best to make our child feel loved and held, and also encourage her age-appropriate steps toward independence. And through all the stages of her growth we endeavor to pay the right amount of loving attention, willingly and wisely.

BOYS AND GIRLS

Our Western culture de-emphasizes the differences between genders, yet anyone who has parented both boys and girls knows that the differences are significant. Those differences require us to attend sensitively to the unique style and needs of boy children and girl children respectively. As women, what a boy child has to teach us about the opposite gender and show us about our relationship to that gender is invaluable. Likewise, a girl child will reflect to us our own gender disposition and the nature of our relationship to the same sex. A father too can learn from the gender differences of his children in this way.

Gender generalizations certainly have some drawbacks. Not every child or grownup can be made to fit the definition. At the same time, to *not* acknowledge the real differences is a disservice. We run the risk of erring on one side or the other of the argument whenever we open the topic. The only solution, or resolution, is to do our own research. If we really pay attention and sharpen our sensitivity to each child's emotional and physical disposition, we can verify what's true about the distinction between boys and girls, and discard what is not useful.

Boys

Pure vitality and instinctive aggression seem to be the natural expression of most boys. As mothers we may have to build our appreciation and understanding of these qualities. We mothers may find ourselves disconcerted and threatened by the sheer volume and intensity of boy's play, while fathers will generally find those same qualities no problem. In my own case, my reaction to my son's temperament was a significant obstacle to maintaining the all-important flow of love and acceptance from me to him. In his later childhood years I have had to do some intentional "catch-up" in this department. The more I have built my stamina for and appreciation of him, the more I've been able to be there for him.

Learning to be sensitive to how a boy ticks and how best to serve him is a worthy pursuit. On one hand, boys require firm boundaries (even in the face of their vitality and aggression), and on the other, lots of space and support to be who they are even if we don't "grok" it. That means we have to figure out how to give them appropriate limits without squashing their essential nature. With boys, we will usually have to expand our comfort zone to include the healthy expression of masculine vitality and aggression. We'll have to deal with a reasonable amount of noise and with the fact that a boy's preferred way to settle an argument is generally with the use of force. When my son and daughter fight, she uses hurtful words and he uses his fists.

Girls

"Moody but more mature" is how I would characterize the girls I know. My daughter can get into fiercely foul moods. As her family we know and suffer those moods more than anyone else. She can be truly scornful and nasty. When she is, her brother is sorely tempted to punch her,

21

and at those times I can sympathize with his reaction. Her emotional responses are her defense in the same way that physical force is his. Her moods are a cover for and clue to the activity going on in her inner world. It can be challenging to stay with her when a girl child is doing her best to "throw" you with her emotional expression. If we can hang in there with her in the right way, we will generally be rewarded with new insight into the mystery of human nature – hers and ours.

On the other side of the coin, girls can be so easy. In general, girls seem to be better than boys at entertaining themselves constructively and at learning earlier and more thoroughly how to take care of themselves. On school mornings my daughter dresses, brushes her hair and teeth, and packs her knapsack before presenting herself in the kitchen for breakfast. Because she is my second child, I gave her the space to do for herself, more than I did for my son. But also she *likes* to take care of things, including herself. Girls can be quietly busy and self-sufficient for much of their day.

Conversely, girl children really tend to thrive on lots of physical affection. The downfall to a girl's tendency to self-sufficiency is that a parent may feel relieved that she isn't demanding, and neglect to give her proper love and attention. A girl child who doesn't feel loved or attended to spells trouble down the line when the adolescent years arrive. Her unfulfilled need for love and attention may then take a self-destructive turn. If we don't want our daughters "looking for love in all the wrong places," as the song goes, we must be sure to give our attention and love in full measure during childhood.

Every human quality has light and dark, positive and negative aspects. Both aspects have much to teach us. Although we may be tempted to label the gender differences as negatives, they are not. My son's vitality is the current of his being from which arises his inquisitiveness, creativity, and brightness. From out of his masculine aggression arises his physical talent and strength, and his courage. My daughter's moodiness is an indication of her emotional sensitivity. I have been astounded by her mature capacity to express love and compassion. She is steady and cheerful in her willingness and ability to do the daily duties she has set for herself, like making her bed and watering the flowers.

Good Company

When our children are young, if we are parenting as practice there is little that is more important than attending to their needs and wants. That can be hard on the adults in our world. I have a few friends with whom I don't spend a lot of time because they compete with my kids for my attention. That creates a difficult situation. While I attempt to respond to my children's needs I am pulled on by the adult to do the same for them.

The kind of adult company that is welcome to the conscious parent is someone who will treat our children with the same respect, attention and interest they accord an adult. This kind of person will typically notice what is needed when in the company of children, and proceed to engage conversation, play a game, or make a friendly boundary with a child when it is called for. Such ideal company frees up the conscious mother or father because the other adult recognizes the child as the parent's priority and participates with her in attending that child, instead of pulling his or her attention in another direction. An adult who can keep company with a parent and child in this way is a rare find.

The best and most natural company when our children are young (under six) is likely to be other parents of young children. Assuming the children are relatively harmonious, parents can enjoy camaraderie and constructive conversation with one another while their kids play. I'm not advocating that we restrict ourselves only to the company of other parents. A friend whose lifestyle is utterly different than ours can be a breath of fresh air. Such a one may provide insight and overview to our situation (and we to theirs) like no other. The qualification for "good company" is someone who can allow the conscious parent's attention to go to her children as needed. We may find ourselves avoiding the company of anyone unwilling or unable to surrender their attention in this way.

In the same way, it would be unwise to encourage playmates our child does not enjoy, or those who are abusive or lacking in reasonable boundaries. Without being overly rigid with our standards for good company, we may have to sacrifice the company of an adult we enjoy if their child falls into the foregoing category.

Having a policy to keep good company is a way of respecting our children and ourselves. When we keep company with people who support our parenting practice, we build on that practice, rather than breaking it down in a struggle to hold our own with those who are ignorant of, or even hostile toward, our intentions.

BOUNDARIES
The 3rd Basic

On a recent shopping expedition to a local department store, I was browsing through the boys department looking for a baseball cap for my son when I heard the wails of a child nearby and coming closer. "If you don't buy me a toy, I'm gonna die!" was the tearful lament. Soon after, a mother with two children came into view. Her older child, riding on the outside of the shopping cart, continued to wail loudly and with feeling that she was going to die if her mother did not buy her a toy. She accused her mother of promising to buy her a toy and now saying no. Her anguished and tear-stained face was turned pleadingly up at her mother.

Notoriously, grocery stores and department stores are places where unconscious acts of child abuse are perpetrated every day. However, this mother was responding to her child with a calm, kind voice; although from the look on her face when they moved into view, I could see this was not the best part of her day. Tuning into the mother's words, I heard her explain to her daughter that she wasn't going to buy her a toy even if she felt like she was going to die. She offered her child a snack and a tube of lip balm, but held her ground on the toy. The little girl tearfully turned down all options, although her crying was quieter now in response to her mother's calm and firm manner.

Empathizing with this mother's position (dealing with a tantruming child in a public place), I lingered nearby wanting to offer her support in a difficult moment. She noticed me watching and gave me a questioning glance. Was I critical of her not giving in to a child so vocally unhappy? I took a step nearer and said, "You're doing good, Mom. Hang in there." She gave me a sudden grateful smile and they moved off to get into a checkout line. Her child's wails had stopped.

Every child needs boundaries or limits to develop optimally. The boundaries on a child's world make it a safe place to grow and learn. Proper boundaries not only guard the physical safety of our children but also teach them respectful (and safe) relationship to their world and the people and things in it. A child who is given the necessary limits can relax and expand within their wise constraint.

The most basic level of boundary-making has to do with physical safety. At this level, the limits we enforce demonstrate to our child that we won't allow them to hurt themselves or others. A child who gets the proper "safety boundaries" learns that they can trust their world because they can trust us. The secondary level of boundary-making has to do with learning right action in relationship to others. These boundaries teach our kids right relationship to the world around them and the people and things in it. So in a sense, this secondary level is training for children to become trustworthy themselves.

For a boundary to be effective it needs to be consistent and understandable to a child's mind. That doesn't mean a boundary can't communicate subtlety, only that it needs to be given in terms comprehensible to a child. There are age-appropriate limits. Trying to keep a busy toddler seated at the dinner table until everyone is finished eating doesn't recognize his biological imperative to move and explore. At this age a child is incapable of observing the social etiquette of mealtime. However, just because that same child likes to drop or throw food over the side of his highchair, doesn't mean he should be allowed to do so. Learning that food is for eating, not throwing, is an age-appropriate boundary for a toddler.

For boundary-making to be effective, it must not be arbitrary. The conscious parent intends to hold only those boundaries that serve to teach a child and/or guard his safety. Enforcing limits that serve no real purpose will just stifle a child's spirit. If we are intending to parent as practice, we will need to develop the ability to make boundaries with objectivity – free of our own unconscious agendas. Our own clarity is key. If we are confused or unsure, the boundary won't stick. Thus it's best to confine ourselves to holding the ones we are sure of. If we're smart we'll work unstintingly on getting clear about both the arbitrary boundaries we may be imposing, and the boundaries we have a hunch we *should* be holding, but can't. Setting arbitrary limits will eventually lead to all-out revolt from a child. Such a child will feel unfairly thwarted and rightfully angry about it. Conversely we may think we do our children a favor by "going easy" on them about boundaries, but it's really no favor at all, just a tremendous disservice. Stating a limit and then backing down on it engenders confusion in the short run and rebellion over the long haul. The confusion at the outset requires a child to retest the boundary. If confusion still reigns, resistance to *all* of our limits will be seeded. If over time we are still generally confused or fearful about giving boundaries, the sprout will become a full-grown weed. And every gardener knows the weeds have the strongest roots.

We may wonder why we need or want to give children boundaries. When the time comes for the first simple limits to be given, they signal the beginning of our child's *training* in life. Young creatures of all kinds must be trained. They are not born knowing their limits. They *do* have an instinctive sense of what limits they need, and when, but the adult of the species must supply them. That adult has presumably been through the training already and has the experience to give this new being what it needs.

Human beings need agreed upon and wise rules for living. Otherwise living together would be impossible. We have only to spend some time in the company of a boundary-less child to find out just how impossible life can be. For some of us it seems that parenting would be so much "nicer" if we didn't have to make boundaries. Although it might mean less conflict in the short run, in the long run parents are asking for real trouble if they try to skirt the boundary issue. It's really not possible to sit on the fence about it.

To translate the boundless love we feel for our newborn into the necessary limits needed by an active toddler can seem too hard. Considerable effort *is* required to provide the proper boundaries. It can look like we are actually hurting our child in the midst of his reaction to a limit. What is required is a new definition, a new form for our love. It's relatively easy to love abstractly, but with our children we are called upon to get practical about our love right away. With a newborn we deal with diapers, nighttime waking and colic. Fast on the heels of all of that comes the need for boundaries on the questing spirit of the busy toddler.

All this is a pretty tall order for the average adult, yet this is exactly what the sacred task of parenting requires. If we've been snoozing through life, a child is a real wake-up call. The demands of a nine to five job may pale in comparison to the twenty-four-hour-a-day job that is parenting. Not only must we come up with the necessary wise action to meet their growing needs but also we must do so any time, any place, and often when we least expect it. For the spiritual student who becomes a parent, *practice* truly becomes a moment to moment affair, no longer confined to just the meditation hall or the workplace, but encompassing all of life.

When our children are young, simplicity and consistency of rules and boundaries is necessary and most useful. As they grow, the emphasis shifts from boundaries for bodily safety to boundaries with relating to the world around them. Between ages three and five children can begin to learn the proper behavior called for in various situations. Although there are many ways in which we must still be the guardian of children's bodily safety, they are also old enough to understand, for instance, the etiquette of mealtime. A child this age would be expected to stay seated while eating her meal, but would then be free to go play quietly in another room. The expectation that mother or father will leave the table with the child has changed. The three-to-five-year-old is able to wait until her parents have finished their meal.

The kind of consistency that is most important in placing limits on children is consistency of context. Because life and human interaction are not so predictable or linear, there are times when boundary-making can *look* inconsistent in form, but consistency of context is maintained. For instance, if a family eats a vegetarian diet and friends come to lunch and bring salami, the guests would not be prohibited from eating the meat. In such an instance, the rules of hospitality to a guest take precedence over the rules of daily diet kept for the vegetarian family.

Furthermore, there is not one right way to handle each situation. In the example above, we might also explain to our guest that our family observes a vegetarian diet and ask them not to serve the meat. Or we could say nothing and simply not eat the meat ourselves. The best way to handle each circumstance is to do what feels right at the time. When my children and I found ourselves in this situation one day, our guest *asked* if we ate meat. When I said we didn't, she left the salami in the kitchen rather than bringing it to the table. Her child wandered into the kitchen, found the salami and ate it. My kids didn't really even think about the salami because it wasn't on the table. Later, my daughter went to the park with our guest and her children and happily ate a snack of salami and grapes with them. Although it is our practice to *not* eat meat, the choice to keep a vegetarian diet is not a moral one for our family. Eating fresh, whole foods and little or no animal flesh just seems to be the optimal way to nourish the body. Since I wasn't there to make a "ruling" on what she should do when salami was available to eat, my daughter did what she wanted to do or what seemed most natural in the situation. Thus we see that personal style and the needs of each situation dictate how boundaries are handled. Too much rigidity, like too little consistency, does not serve a child's life training.

Older children can also learn boundaries as they pertain to right relationship to the natural world. If they see that we refrain from littering garbage, or take only the amount of food we can eat at a meal, our children will learn by our example. Setting limits also comes into play in the give and take of social relationship with family and friends. A younger child, for instance, will grab, scratch or even bite to get a toy he wants. Older children can begin to appreciate the value of cooperation with playmates and the mutual pleasure that comes with sharing a toy or game together.

When we traveled to India with our children, I was amazed at how quickly they learned the cultural etiquette around eating. Not only did they learn to eat proficiently with their hands (*right* hand only in India), but they also adapted quite well to the distinctive spicing and preparation of foods both familiar and foreign, while fending off our insistent hosts who pressed huge quantities of food on them in keeping with the norms of Indian hospitality.

Children can learn sensitivity to spaces both ordinary (like the dinner table) and sacred (like a church). With ordinary spaces that can mean noticing what is happening

31

and/or the mood present when they enter a room or join a group of people. Children can tell the difference between quiet and noisy. They can see that everyone is listening to one person speak or that several conversations are happening at once. With sacred spaces a child's training can be as simple as learning to respect a parent's meditation time, or as complex as knowing the correct behavior expected during a religious and/or sacred ceremony in a church, synagogue or Hindu temple.

The boundary-making (or maybe we should call it *distinction* making) of instructing our children in sensitivity to people and spaces is *not* about teaching them to be well behaved so we aren't embarrassed. It's not that children are essentially ignorant or insensitive. It's about respecting children enough to give them a wise orientation to life – an orientation that we may have to acquire in order to have it to give. That's what the sacred task of parenting requires of us. The conscious parent is concerned with preserving the wonder and innocence inherent in children, and in all life, by the way she relates to children and by how and what she teaches. Boundary-making with older children is not about preaching to them or shaming children about what they don't know. It's also not about indoctrinating them into our worldview or our beliefs in order to make them carbon copies of us. Instead, giving our children a wise orientation to life with our boundary-making ideally provides them with a sane framework upon which to build a life of their own design.

The value for us in this whole process is that we can acquire genuine wisdom, and regain our wholeness when we learn to provide wise guidance to our children. It can look and feel like "give, give, give" from us to our child. And the form of things *is* that, especially at the start. But in that giving we are also getting. *We* get a training in how to provide the "parent half" of the parent-child relationship.

In an earlier time it may have been a foregone conclusion that a parent would already have the training required for the job of raising children. Why don't we as parents seem to have the needed tools today? Why has our upbringing been so lacking? Many of us find ourselves practically clueless in relationship to children. A full consideration of those questions is probably the material for another book, but it is clearly a different world today than it was a generation ago. The stress of our times creates unique demands on our parenting. The model of parenting of a previous era ("children should be seen and not heard," and "spare the rod and spoil the child") is mercifully no longer the norm. But we are often at a loss for what to replace it with. The reality is that we must invent the new formula. There is a wonderful world of possibility in that task. Inevitably we will make mistakes in our experimentation with new solutions.

On the other hand, what makes a good parent today is the same thing that has always made a good parent. A good parent is a mature adult who can practice kindness, generosity and compassion toward children. Such a parent will experiment to find the proper blend of love and discipline required to raise a child wisely.

REASONABLE EXPRECTATIONS

To have reasonable expectations of our children is an important aspect of wise boundary-making. Reasonable expectations leave room for a child to be a child. All too often I find myself trying to hold my kids to a standard of behavior that would be challenging for most adults to live up to! So many struggles with our children could be avoided by adjusting our expectations. I used to try to nap when my children were home and they would never leave me alone for more than a few minutes. Because of their ages, and the way I raised them, it was not something they could do. I'd feel frustrated because I wasn't getting to rest, and my kids would feel anxious or undirected until I was done. I finally realized that if I needed to nap it would have to happen when my children either weren't home or were in the care of my husband or a babysitter.

Children *do* have the possibility to grow up to be more mature than the adults who raise them, so it's important to teach to their highest potential. We can aim to educate them in genuine human maturity while at the same time being careful to have our expectations for their behavior commensurate with their age, personality and environment. Sensible expectations allow parent and child to relax, gracefully creating the space for a child's natural progression to maturity under the wise guidance of his or her parents.

Work

At our house we do not have an equal division of household chores. I prefer to do everything my way and I have a hard time leaving anything for anybody else to do. Then I complain that I have too much to do and blame my family for not helping out. But there is value in teaching children to be able to "do" for themselves. With experience I am developing the patience to teach my children and really enjoy it. For the most part, both of my children are highly capable and willing workers.

Children, especially at a certain age, naturally want to do for themselves and help adults with the tasks of daily living. If we are careful not to squelch that natural movement, and patient in our instruction of them, we should not have to force children to pull their own weight as they get older. Up to this point we have not made our kids do assigned chores. Our approach has been to strongly model the desired behaviors by our example, and to ask for our children's cooperation and assistance along the way. When they say yes to such requests, I feel pleased and satisfied. When they say no, I struggle with anger and annoyance and the question of how much to allow children their preferences. Overall, the mood that feels right is to invite them to help rather than require it. Forcing them to do tasks seems heavy-handed.

Recently my son had to collect pledges for a Little League Hit-A-Thon. The idea of the event was to get friends and family to commit to pay so many cents for every foot the child hit the baseball in the best out of three hits. On the day before the Hit-A-Thon, I was out dutifully collecting pledges on my child's behalf, when it suddenly occurred to me that he ought to be soliciting some of them himself. He felt shy about asking people for money, even people highly likely to say yes. I could understand that because I felt the same way. Furthermore he was grumpy about taking part in the event at all. I told him that I had collected six pledges for him and was now proposing that he collect the next few. That seemed like a reasonable expectation and I believe it was.

When his response was one of resistance, I pushed harder and soon he and I were locking horns. The boundary was a good one, but there was heated emotion in my follow through. I felt fearful that my child would never learn to speak for himself, and that translated into the rigid determination that he ought to begin to learn *now*. I neglected to consider the important natural consequence of him not speaking up for himself to collect more pledges. He would have fewer names on his pledge card, but also learn an invaluable lesson about the nature of work. That evening my husband spoke to our son and expressed his support of the expectation that he collect some of his own pledges. My husband lovingly but firmly pointed out that the idea of the Hit-A-Thon was for the *kids* to get the pledges, not the parents. He explained that we all have things we feel uncomfortable or resistant to doing, and the way we get to see that we *can* do them is by going ahead even though we don't want to. Sure enough, by the time his dad had finished explaining the truth of the situation to him, including acknowledging our son's mixed feelings about the Hit-A-Thon, he looked down at his pledge card and said excitedly, "I could have filled this thing up!" The next day our son had a grand time at the baseball event and left saying, "Next time I'm gonna get lots of names!"

Several days later I was returning home after picking up the kids from a swim party. As I reflected on the wet suits and soggy towels being carried into the house, I realized I was unwilling to have them left in a heap at my feet. My kids were the ones who just spent the afternoon playing and swimming. Wasn't it time they also had the experience of taking care of wet pool gear when the playing was done? It was fresh in my mind that the way I had attempted to make a boundary over the Hit-A-Thon pledges had not been successful. In a moment of inspiration I asked, "Can I show you two where to hang your wet gear to dry?" The wording and the mood were just right. I didn't ask if they *wanted* to hang up their stuff, I asked if I could show them *where* to hang it. My mood was soft and inviting. They both responded positively although my son asked if I could show him later because he had something to do in his room first. Of course, *my* way is to take care of wet gear right away, but I realized it really made no difference if it was done immediately or not. "Okay," I answered. "Tell me when you're ready for me to show you." Half an hour later he told me he was ready to hang his stuff and would I show him where?

There really is no one right way to raise our children to be responsible, and the best way is the one we parents can get behind. Until or unless we become convicted of another way, we do best to stick to what we feel is the right way, not out of stubborn ignorance, but as a way of being in integrity with ourselves and honoring our own process of growth and evolution. However, any method of making boundaries or instilling responsibility that is shaming or disrespectful of our children is ultimately a failure even if it gets "results" in the short term. In such a scenario what is actually learned is the *way* the lesson was taught, not the specifics of the lesson.

FOOD
The 4th Basic

This chapter will cover not only what nurtures the body of our child, but also what nurtures her soul. Children begin to "feed" in utero. They feed on the emotional and physical world inside mother, and outside her as it filters through her body. But mostly, in utero they are as fully taken care of, without our having to think about it, as they are ever going to be. A woman's body has the complete blueprint for the job. A mother has only to tend to her emotional well being, eat enough of the right foods and get adequate sleep. That can seem like a lot, especially if she already has other children in her care. But really, it's basic.

Once a child is born, mother must *actively* feed her baby the literal and subtle food he or she needs. If a child is nursed when hungry, the "literal" aspect of feeding is taken care of. But we also provide our child with impression food in the form of how we touch, speak to, and even *think* about, him. The emotional climate into which an infant is received is a form of "food." A newborn's main activities are eating and sleeping (and crying). They "eat" milk and impressions, and then sleep to digest both the milk and the impressions. Under the heading of the food "basic," we can consider not only nursing and solid food, but also touch, shared sleep and environmental impressions as they affect our newborn and older child.

Nursing

After birth, a baby's pristine digestive system is called upon to perform its job for the first time, and like a new iron skillet, the system needs "seasoning." The "seasoning" process will generally be more easeful if the baby's first food is human breast milk, because mother's milk contains elements exactly intended to get the system up and running properly. However, a new infant's digestion will typically give him some trouble no matter whether there is breast milk or formula running through it. At one time or another babies will experience gas, bloating, diarrhea and/or constipation. As a parent, we do our best to alleviate the discomfort of our little one and leave it to nature and time to do the "seasoning" required.

Although the majority of mothers choose to bottle-feed, I would whole-heartedly recommend breast-feeding over bottle-feeding. Having nursed both my children, it amazes me that any woman who *could* nurse would choose not to. Many women don't have the information or support they would need to nurse their child. Others choose bottle-feeding because it allows them more freedom from their child. A nursing mother must keep fairly constant company with her infant to be available for feedings, or else pump breast-milk to be left for her baby if she has to be away. Truthfully, many women *must* work and cannot afford the "luxury" of staying at home with their infant. I am still convinced of the rightness and convenience of nursing, and saddened that more mothers aren't willing or able to engage this very natural and womanly act. To hold my child close and nourish her with milk from my body, as nature intended, always gave me a marvelous feeling of well-being and contentment, and increased my love for that helpless little being in my arms.

In our sanitized culture here in the West, we have a confused notion about natural body functions and sexuality. We often mistake anything to do with the body as being sexual. The average Western woman sees her breasts as part of her sexual equipment. Her breasts are attractive to the opposite sex. Her breasts are fondled on her first "heavy" date. Her sexual partner may suck or lick them during sex. Special brassieres are made that push up one's breasts so even the more modestly endowed woman can have cleavage. But here's something to think about. The reason breasts play a part in the mating game is because they have the literal capacity to nurture life. That's an attraction so obvious to our primitive ancestors and so lost on most of us that the fact that we never thought of it that way may be shocking.

A mother who is bottle-feeding, either by necessity or choice, will want to be sure her infant is getting enough "in-arms" time, resisting the convenient temptation to prop the baby up somewhere with the bottle while she goes on about other business. Expectant mothers who would like to nurse but don't know where to begin, can consult the phonebook or use the internet to locate the nearest chapter of the La Leche League, a national organization that supports and educates women about breastfeeding. I was lucky enough to have a lot of support and good role modeling from women I knew who breastfed their children. Without that, I may not have nursed my children. The example and support of other women who breastfed was of more practical value to me than all the information I read about why to nurse. For the purposes of this book, I'm going to assume the reader either nurses, or is sympathetic to that practice.

In the idyllic early phase of a baby's life, the food issue is pretty relaxed and natural. We nurse our baby when she's hungry, lull her to sleep in our arms, wear her on our body, and all is right with the world. Yes, we must wake up with her in the night when we'd rather be deeply asleep. Yes, we must bear the frustration of not knowing what she needs because she can't tell us in words. Yes, the enforced intimacy of being in nearly constant physical contact with this little being is not always welcome. Still, there is the overall bodily sensing that what we are doing is right and there is deep fulfillment in that.

The next stage of feeding involves the joyous, sensuous discovery of solid food. It often begins with a luscious piece of fruit. When my son was a baby he was sitting in my lap while I ate a ripe purple plum. I had taken one bite, exposing the sweet juicy inner flesh. When I wasn't looking he latched onto the bitten side of the fruit and starting sucking with rapture. His innocent passion for that yummy plum made me laugh with delight. After the first encounter, a child goes on to explore many more foods (the more natural the better!), and we begin to see that food for him is not just something that goes into the mouth. It's also something to squeeze between his fingers and smash on the table. He may drop food over the side of his high-chair or fling it across the room. All such activity is a part of the joy of food, and also a quite serious "scientific" exploration of his world. *Amazing how that lump of food fell down onto the floor. Let me try that again…* Which is not to say that I think it's a good idea to allow a child to throw or otherwise waste food. Just don't be too attached to every bite of food going directly into his mouth.

Once solid food has been introduced or discovered, the nursing relationship begins to gradually shift from being essential to life to being more a form of emotional nurturance. We nurse to augment our child's solid food intake, to maintain our mutual bond, and to serve as our child's ground of being and source of comfort and love. In another two years, our child may run to us with a scraped knee or an emotional upset and want to nurse. At first it will be right to do that, and more and more as children grow we will wean them of this form of comfort. Nursing will not be the universal solution it once rightly was. Many women wean their child at two or three years old. I nursed my first child for two and one-half years and my second child for five. Any amount of nursing is better than not nursing at all. The shorter the span of time a child nurses, the quicker will be the cycle from nursing for sustenance, to nursing for comfort and connection, to weaning.

Once our child begins to eat solid food, she may enjoy eating from our plate, even when we're both eating the same thing. At a particular point both my kids preferred to drink from my water bottle when we were out in the car, even though they each had water bottles of their own. This desire to share our food is simply a natural extension of the nursing relationship. It will end when there is no longer a need for its expression in that form.

Fresh and Whole

The children I know, my own and others, are all at times more or less finicky about food. Toddlers who nurse may go through phases where they eat more solid food and nurse less or vice versa. Sometimes we may wonder if they'll ever make that shift over to solid food. When nursing days are over, and a child is eating all solid food, his likes and dislikes begin to assume greater importance. When children are young, if we feed them fresh whole food they will eat nearly everything. It's beneficial to feed children foods in their most natural form, because this early diet lays the foundation for their lifetime eating habits. That's a serious responsibility for a parent.

As our children grow, they exhibit both natural and learned preferences for some foods over others. If those predilections have to do with unprocessed foods, I would allow the child to eat what they are attracted to. But even very young children will choose sugary or processed foods over whole foods like fruits and vegetables. We must direct them to a healthy diet if that's what we want them to eat.

As a general guideline, it's valuable to keep kids eating as much of a variety of fresh and whole foods as possible. But even if they only eat two broccoli spears along with their pile of spaghetti, they'll keep their taste for the kinds of foods that are the best fuel for their bodies. Fresh whole foods are appealing and good to eat and when children are offered these foods regularly, they get the ongoing experience of how their body responds to such foods, as compared with the response to processed foods. We all need those reminders. It's so easy to let the attractive taste of fast foods be our guide and just get used to living with the negative effects of these foods on our body. I look for occasions to have natural food be the only option. For instance, if I am going out for an afternoon of shopping with my kids, I will take apples, rice cakes and almond butter in a cooler. If the children beg for processed foods they see while we're out, I can say no to the pizza or ice cream and offer the food I brought. If they are genuinely hungry, they'll eat what we have.

It is also important to not be over controlling or obsessive about maintaining absolute purity in a child's diet, if that's our leaning. That just creates rigidity in a child's body and mind and doesn't allow her to discover how to make "food" out of whatever she eats. Ideally children develop a relationship to the full range of possible foods to eat with an emphasis on the fresh and whole: fruit and vegetables, whole grains, beans, and nuts and seeds. For more information on how to eat this way, Lalitha Thomas's book *Ten Essential Foods* is an excellent resource (see bibliography.)

As our children move into the teen years, they will rightfully want to decide what to eat for themselves. At this point, we need to free them up to make more of their own choices, and trust in the good eating habits that we have given them. Once they leave home, of course, our children are fully in charge of their diet. At that point our input on food should only be offered if it is asked for.

IMPRESSION FOOD

We feed our children more than just "meat and potatoes" when we raise them. We also provide an environment for them to grow in that is rich with impressions both positive and negative. These impressions feed our child's growing psyche like meat and potatoes feed their bodies.

Role Modeling

Young children absorb every nuance of their parents' being and character. These impressions are as much "food" for our growing child as their daily diet. That's a daunting prospect to even the most seasoned and confident mom or dad. For a parent, the responsibility of being the most significant role model in the life of a growing child can be sobering. This is sure to be the toughest job any of us ever had. But the parent-child relationship is also an inspiring and delightful chance to be part of the lawful maturation of both our child and us. To raise a child demands we put our best foot forward in order to nurture them with the most optimal impression food. What a wonderful opportunity! On-the-job training doesn't get any better than that!

Role modeling is a matter of *who we are* rather than *how we parent*. That's the good news *and* the bad news. The good news is that we don't have to pretend to be or act like anyone other than who we really are. The bad news is that we can't select what our kids absorb from us. Even if we feel okay about the "face" we show the world, our child has access not only to that public face, but to all the other faces we try not to show. Our children and partners reflect back to us those unacceptable faces of ours. That means we get to see the full range of who we are, which can be disturbing. Yet it's only those aspects of ourselves that we are blind to or ignorant of that are troublesome. To be a wise role model to a child doesn't require that we be perfect. Which is a good thing because otherwise we'd never measure up! To role model as a mother or father simply requires us to be aware of our foibles and willing to work on them. Our workability with our shortcomings is some of the best kind of impression food for our children.

Unconscious habits and beliefs are the kinds of impression food we ought to be aware of because they are precisely the behaviors a child absorbs so readily. We may have the habit of complaining when things don't go our way, or of overeating, or perhaps of speaking disrespectfully to our marriage partner. We may have the belief that others are always criticizing us, or we may have racial or cultural prejudice against anyone different from us, or we may unconsciously believe that every time a child cries we need to "fix" it. These are common shortcomings or character flaws that typically have deep roots in the psyche. We may not be able to change these aspects of our character overnight or even ever, but we can certainly curb our expression of them and/or be able to openly admit to them, especially with our children.

In the same way that children will illuminate for us the less-than-optimal impression food we provide, they also show us the positive impression food we give them with our gifts and talents. Their innocence and delight naturally expand our being and we shine through, perhaps like never before. If we have something good to model for a child, we ought to put it out there – not in a conceited way, but with confidence in its inherent value. Perhaps we have a skill like acting, horseback riding or baseball. We may lead our child in some form of that activity, or simply give them the chance to witness us demonstrate our talent. Of equal (or even greater) value would be to show a child interpersonal skills (impression food) such as the ability to admit when we've made a mistake and apologize, or the ability to help two people solve a heated conflict.

Even the difficult or challenging moments (or hours!) in the company of children can be a blessing when the circumstance draws out our strength or wisdom as a role model. Precisely because parenting is likely to be one of the most rigorous jobs we ever undertake, we will want to provide the best of impression food in relationship to our children. When our child is struggling to understand and accept the natural or defined limits of his reality, it can be difficult for a parent. We may be looking at a squirming, screaming toddler in full tantrum mode on the floor, or dealing with deadly looks and a slammed door from our teenager. Although we will likely mishandle the difficult moments many times, on those occasions when we rise to them with our best side it is to the betterment of all concerned.

Throughout my years of parenting, whenever either one of my kids had a problem I couldn't "fix," I generally made the assumption that I had screwed up somehow, which would cause me to feel mad or scared, or both. Those feelings inclined me to either get tough or wimp out, neither one of which provided very good impression food. My pre-teen has recently been going through a very emotional time. He has been weepy and anxious for no obvious reason. On one occasion I was comforting my distraught child while struggling with my own feelings, when I found myself unexpectedly attuned to his being. I understood how he was feeling and saw him for what he is right now – a vulnerable, sensitive young boy who often feels helpless in an adult world to which he has yet to be given "the keys." I immediately softened from my stance of anger and fear and, although I still couldn't "fix it," at least I knew how to be emotionally available to my son in his struggle.

Mercifully our children seem to naturally see us for who we are. They are infinitely forgiving and loving with us. In this way, they feed us on the truth of our situation. We do well to follow their lead in this regard and ease up on ourselves for their sake and ours. If we can do that, we will be giving a child the very best kind of impression food there is.

Reading Together

Reading together is food for the imagination. Our children have been raised without television or computers and only occasional movies. Our leisure time is spent with, among other things, books. We typically begin and end the day with the reading aloud of written stories. Although our kids are old enough now to read to themselves and often do, we still preserve the tradition of daily reading together because we are all so "fed" by it. Our morning and evening reading sessions are the perfect opportunity to snuggle and hug in a heap under the reading lamp. We read from a variety of materials that are both entertaining and educational. My aim is to nourish their young minds and hearts by exposing them to other cultures and ways of being as well as to reinforce human virtues like courage and kindness. As they have gotten older and their attention span has increased, we sometimes even read non-fiction selections on history or science.

At times our reading sessions become for the children a lazy way to get me to entertain them. The cues that they are treating me like a television set are a demanding tone of voice, loud complaints when I announce the end of our reading time (okay, they nearly *always* complain when it's time to stop, but they sometimes complain more cantankerously than usual), general fussiness and claims to be "so bored," and so on. When this happens, I figure it's time for a different activity, or for each of them to spend some time alone occupying themselves.

I am pleased to observe that our children have become avid readers. I often find one or both of them sprawled on the bed, or in the corner on top of the heat vent utterly absorbed, reading a book. Sometimes we all read our own books together in the same room. I feel good about having raised my kids on a diet of good literature at a time when the written word seems in some danger of going out of vogue, especially with young people who have been raised on television and computers as their primary forms of entertainment.

Feeding Ourselves

During the exploratory phase of toddlerhood when we are busy keeping our child out of harms way, we may literally lack the time to eat. Mealtimes are often disrupted by a two-year-old on the go who is ready to resume his exploratory "work" after about three to five minutes of eating. Since children of this age are generally not safe when unattended and out of sight, the conscientious mom or dad will follow their youngster, perhaps with dinner plate in hand, or with their meal left unfinished for the moment. In either case, dinnertime will not be what it was before baby. It is important to keep ourselves well-nourished, but regular mealtimes may not be the best time for that. Just before or after the formal mealtime, or when our child is sleeping and refueling for the next round of exploration, may be better. With a little creativity and flexibility we can manage to keep ourselves well fed. If possible, it's nice to have someone else care for our child on occasion – a babysitter or friend – so that mom and dad can enjoy an undisturbed meal together. But how do we get the nourishment we need beyond the food we put in our mouths?

From birth to about six years of age, the task of raising a child dominates our energy and attention. Thus it's not uncommon for parents, especially mothers, to feel depleted and run down. We get so busy and focused on serving our growing child that as an adult who was perhaps not so good at attending to her own genuine needs *before* she had children, we may really hit bottom. We're sleep-deprived, underfed, and can't remember the last time we were alone with our husband. The house is a mess and the idea of spaciousness and relaxation with our children seems as distant as the next star in the galaxy. The thing we probably most need and crave is exactly what we are unlikely to get right now, and that is, the time to feed our heart and soul. And yet, it is crucial that we do our best to arrange for exactly that.

The overriding theme of parenting is, of course, sacrifice of our needs for our child's. That said, the conscious parent sees the larger need to keep themselves intact and growing so that they are *able* to put their children first. Whether the "soul food" we need is literally prayer and meditation (and those come highly recommended), or tending the garden, if we make the time for what feeds us, we'll definitely reap the benefits. It's probably wise to figure on giving ourselves fairly exclusively to our child for the first two years of his life. After that we may judiciously take time away from parenting to pursue the kinds of activities that feed us. Although it often seems a razor's edge to balance what's best for our child with what's best for us, the struggle to find that balance in our parenting is a decidedly worthy endeavor.

Touch
The 5th Basic

Animal studies have shown, rather dramatically, the need of all living things for touch and love in order to grow and prosper. Perhaps the best known of these studies, those of Harlow, involved baby monkeys being separated from their mothers at birth. Deprived of loving touch, these babies would attempt to get comfort by rocking themselves and self-stimulating. When they grew older their behavior was asocial and violent. All was definitely *not* well in the absence of touch.

So it goes with our children. They too need contact for their health and wellbeing. No matter our disposition or conditioning, we must find a way to give our children loving touch. Differences in the physical expression of affection are to be expected. Some people are just more naturally reserved about touch while others are quite comfortable with lots of contact. Touch is connection and as such it transcends the physical. We can "touch" one another with a loving gaze or tone of voice. On the other hand there is something utterly natural and organic about the need for and response to loving physical touch. It is beyond mind and reason. At times when I have had the presence of mind and attention to notice what we both need, I have simply gathered my fussy, angry or tired child in my arms. Giving up on "working it out" verbally or reasonably with him or her (at least for the moment), I put my trust in touch. So often it is the missing ingredient.

Nature intends for babies to be held. Before birth, a child is held securely and continuously in the organic embrace of his mother's body. A newborn's standard for touch is the warm enclosure of the womb. A child is born when the more delicate machinery of the physical body (heart, lungs and brain), is ready to run, and when the infant needs more room to continue its growth process. The world outside the womb indeed gives a child the needed space, but mother's arms provide all the additional room needed for some months. A newborn's eyesight extends only as far as her mother's face. Mother's embrace provides the newborn with an essential sense of safety and connection in a brand new world of sights and sounds. Even an infant crib no doubt seems a lonely expanse compared to the snug womb.

When my children were babies, I held and carried them on my body whether I felt like it or not. I knew that physical contact is what babies want and need. Still, there's no denying the in-arms phase of a child's life can be challenging in practice. Many things are difficult to do with a baby in-arms. Thinking back, I probably would not have tried to do as much as I felt driven to do then. Or I would have asked for more help. If we are committed to maintaining contact with our child, soft baby-carriers and slings are invaluable at this point. These practical devices, plus a big dose of surrender to our reduced mobility, will get us through those early months. Mercifully, magically, the recognition of the bright blessing of the beautiful child in our arms puts it all in perspective.

It's hard to be *too* physically affectionate with children, especially in infancy, yet there may be times when our expressions of affection are unwelcome. Children are sensitive to being patronized, smothered, or interrupted by touch. As they grow, we do well to recognize that there are other ways to connect with our kids. We can "touch" with our voice, our eyes and our actions. When we speak of being "touched" by someone or something, we are referring to the experience of an opening in the heart. That kind of "touch" is the wellspring of loving connection with our children.

There are natural variations, for children and adults, in the need for touch. Those differences should be honored. But many adults developed their physical reserve in response to a lack of adequate touch in childhood. If we've held our child in-arms as an infant, much of our physical reserve will have been broken through by the time our child is old enough to hurtle herself into our lap with a book to read. A child's unabashed drive for affection and attention is an ongoing reminder of this vital human need.

Shared Sleep

Babies (and their mothers and fathers!) instinctively love to snuggle and be close. Babies are meant to nurse from their mother's breasts and can do so with the greatest ease when mother and child sleep together. A mother who sleeps with her child is naturally more aware of and responsive to her baby's needs than is a mother separated from her baby by walls and doors.

Recent scientific research shows that during sleep an infant relies upon the breathing patterns of adults to regulate his own breathing. Infants must learn to move through the cycles of breathing that occur while awake, while asleep and during the stages of sleep. A baby who sleeps with adults (and whose parents practice "baby-wearing" in the day) can pattern himself off the breathing cycles of the adults, and thus learn more quickly and safely to make the appropriate shifts. Sleeping separately, or not held enough, a baby is entirely on his own to work through breathing transitions. It is now thought by some researchers that SIDS (Sudden Infant Death Syndrome) may be the result of a baby's failure to transition properly through a breathing cycle, in the absence of an adult to pattern from.

Our pioneer ancestors slept together out of necessity. Beds were few and modern central heating unknown. Somewhere along the line, perhaps because we now have the luxury to do so, we got the idea that babies and children should sleep separately from their parents. Now it is commonly believed that sleeping together with our children is harmful. Antagonists of the family bed say that an adult could roll over on their infant and smother it. As a mother who slept with both her babies, I can say that having my infant so close to me actually made me hyper-alert to my baby's presence and needs.

Another argument against co-sleeping is that a baby needs to learn to comfort itself. How on earth an infant could be expected to be able to provide loving touch and comfort to itself is beyond comprehension! (Think of those baby monkeys.) We also hear that a child who sleeps with his or her parents will never learn to separate. Well it *is* true that such a child will fight for the physical closeness to which he or she had become accustomed if it's not yet time for that child to separate. Couples who practice attachment-style parenting must be sure to separate from their children when the time is right. (More on that in Chapter 10, *Holding On/Letting Go*.) Other opponents of the family bed claim that a mother and father are entitled to the privacy of their bedroom and the space for physical intimacy between them. True enough, but whoever imagines that parents don't have to surrender their privacy in the early years of childraising probably never had kids!

Perhaps the strongest argument against co-sleeping is the fear that a child could be not only witness to, but also object of, sexual contact with his parents. Perhaps co-sleeping presupposes a level of basic human maturity that is not common for modern adults, but it would seem that healthy bodily contact and affection between children and their parents would have the effect of eliminating any inclination to inappropriate physical contact with our children. If we have any doubts of our trustworthiness in this domain, seeking professional help is strongly advised. On a related point, Tine Thevenin observes in her book *The Family Bed* (Perigee Books, 1987):

>...in spite of society's preoccupation with separate
>beds and bedrooms, supposedly to guard children

and give them a moral upbringing, sexual promiscuity among teenagers and adults knows almost no limits, even though premarital or extra-marital sexual relations are greatly taboo...This strong interest in sex may be an indirect result of the minimal physical contact that much of the younger generation has received during infancy. Perhaps some inner drive is attempting to repair the damage of too little bodily stimulation during childhood. (p. 109.)

The family bed may actually *prevent* sexual promiscuity in our children by providing them with the physical contact and affection children instinctively seek from their parents.

My husband and I practiced shared sleep with both our children. In fact, our common bed is still the hub of family life for us. We sleep there of course, but also read, work, talk and play games there. At present we are still using a king-sized bed to accommodate our youngest, who dearly loves to cuddle on her mother's arm to fall asleep every night. I must confess that I love it too. I'm still glad to know she's right beside me and that I'll be the first to know if she has a bad dream or a bellyache in the night. I'm not ready for her to be farther away and neither is she. My husband and I periodically remind her that the time will come in the next couple of years when she will begin to sleep on her own. The idea is that she, and we, will know when that should happen, just as we knew when it was time for our son to sleep in his own bed.

As our son grew, even a king-sized bed couldn't accommodate all four of us comfortably. I also had the sense that a physical separation between mother and son for sleep was now appropriate. Having our son wrapped around me in the bed was no longer right as he moved into young boyhood. However, since his departure from the family bed, I look for ways to show appropriate physical affection to him, like hugs and cheek kisses, as often as I can.

Tine Thevenin again comments:

> Sleeping together has a soothing effect on misunderstandings and harsh words spoken during the day. For an average of eight hours, in the stillness of the night, and the relaxing and disarming state of sleep, those who sleep together touch as if to say, "You are all right. I'm all right." We remain in touch with one another. It is such a wonderful feeling to wake up in the middle of the night, and to kiss a loved one while he or she is asleep. (*The Family Bed*, p. 37.)

As with nursing our children, sleeping together acts as a "reset" button at the end of one day and before beginning the next. To have my child or children next to me all night snuggled up or just touching feet or arms makes an organic communication of our connectedness and our mutual "okay"-ness.

The Practicalities of Shared Sleep

Over the years of sleeping in a family bed I've learned a few things. One is that the bed needs to be large enough.

The other is not to let a child get used to sleeping *between* mother and father. If the bed is too small, somebody is going to end up packed in the middle like a sardine in a can. That kind of crowding is not really conducive to a good night's sleep. If the family bed includes just one child, a queen-size mattress works pretty well. But with a growing child, or more than one child in the bed, only a king-size mattress will truly suffice.

My husband and I let our first child get used to sleeping *between* us, and thus many years went by without us being able to cuddle with one another at night. And our son, like many children, kicked off the covers. Children's bodies seem to be naturally warmer than adults, they also seem to resist the confinement of blankets weighing them down when they sleep. The result was that Mom and Dad were separated by a restless ever-growing child sleeping between them. Wistfully we bid one another goodnight over his active little body and then spent the night fighting to keep the blankets over our shivering bodies. Our son fought mightily to maintain his position in the middle. He had become accustomed to it. He had Mom *and* Dad, one on either side. It was a good spot for him, it just didn't work for us. We never were able to really budge him from that spot until he began the transition out of the family bed.

When our daughter came along I established her sleeping position next to me on the outer side of the bed, thus preserving access to my husband at night and giving her room to kick off the covers without taking ours with her. She still sleeps in that spot and she still uses fewer covers than we do. The only downside to the arrangement is my husband's occasional lament that he never gets the opportunity to snuggle with our daughter as she falls asleep. Considering our shared sleep history, perhaps it *was* appropriate for our son to be between us and thus always able to have access to his father during sleep. Maybe a boy needs that. A girl needs her father too, but it has always felt exactly right to have my daughter next to *me* during sleep. She has other occasions to be close with her dad. Now especially, at age seven, it would not feel quite right for her and her dad to cuddle to sleep at night.

In some tribal cultures, women and children sleep in one place and men in another. That configuration does fit the natural order of things. But I have also appreciated, and needed, closeness with my husband at night. I haven't always found it an easy thing to keep our connection intact in the midst of mothering two children. Husband and wife can get lost in the mix. The mothering role is so all-encompassing of time and attention. For husband and wife to be able to lie in one another's arms at night is a wonderful thing. In that way, the adults too can "recharge" from their busy day. Aside from the all-important exchange of touch, those few minutes before we both fall into much needed slumber are sometimes our only chance to catch up on the news of the day and exchange essential information. When we have been unable to have a good talk for awhile, we have occasionally found ourselves awake in the night and spontaneously had an extended and very fulfilling conversation into the wee hours.

Sex and the Family Bed

And what of sexual intimacy and the family bed? How *does* a couple have sex with their kids right there in the same bed? On those occasions when parents want to be sexually intimate in the family bed, they will have to be creative as well as practical. With more than one child in the shared bed, it will probably be necessary to find another spot for sexual activity or move the sleeping babes. If there's just one child and the bed is big enough to accommodate such activity without unduly disturbing that child, then just go for it. That *doesn't* mean having the wildest sex ever and making as much noise as possible without regard for the sleeping child next to us, but sexual intimacy is a very natural function of life. It is good for our children to learn to relate to their body functions without shame and awkwardness. If most of the world shares sleep (and that's what the studies show), then surely most of the world's couples do not have utter privacy in which to be intimate with one another. On occasion this lack of privacy can be a kind of natural birth control and that's well and good. If we are interrupted during sexual intimacy when our child wakes and needs us, then not only are we prevented from completing the physical act of procreation, but we also get an organic reminder of what we are responsible to and for when sexual intimacy results in a child. If the child settles right back down to sleep, then we can carry on with the lovemaking.

To be completely practical, though, at bedtime when it comes to a choice between sleep and sex, especially for exhausted parents, it's usually sleep, or sleepy sex. That can be nice if it's not *too* sleepy. However, intimacy between husband and wife is best arranged, if possible, to happen at an intentional time and place. Look for the time to be intimate together and make the mood. Once the children are old enough we can arrange for them to spend time at a friend's house or take an afternoon together when they are at school. Parents deserve such time together away from their kids, not just for sex, but to talk and dine together without interruption.

At some point in the growth of my children, it stopped being okay to have sex in the same bed or room with them. I can't say exactly when that was, except that it seemed roughly coincident with the time when each child was ready to sleep in his own bed. My husband and I both had a tacit recognition of the need to use another room and to redouble efforts to transition that child to his own bed for sleep. As wonderful and right as it is to share sleep with our children when they are young, it is of equal importance to recognize when it's time for our children to sleep separately and to help them make that transition.

The Marriage Relationship

The reality of the busy life of parents is that we don't always remember to honor our adult need for touch and sexual intimacy with one another. Sexual intimacy between man and woman is an important part of married life. Sexuality (and the possibility of having children) is what distinguishes the friendship of marriage from ordinary friendship. Married "friends" are obligated to feed that aspect of their friendship because it's an integral part of their connection. No matter how tired or *not* in the mood a couple may feel it's important to maintain sexual contact with one another. If we are willing to go beyond limiting thought patterns or emotional moods that say "Not tonight," we can start out just going through the motions, and end up having a very pleasurable, even transcendent, encounter with one another. Furthermore, couples who respect the primacy of their relationship with each other have the proper orientation from which to parent with balance and maturity.

Holding

Because many parents did not receive enough touch in their own childhood experience, and because parenting is a demanding, sometimes exhausting job no matter how much touch we did or didn't get, "holding" for adults is a wonderful way to receive nourishment and encouragement from a friend. Although we may have a strong and satisfying sexual relationship with our husband or wife, the kind of holding I speak of here feeds the "child" inside each of us who may long to be held and accepted like a baby in non-sexual, intentionally nurturing embrace. I don't suggest this as a casual activity but rather one done with the specific intent to "reset" the person being held so that their essential goodness is affirmed for them.

Holding is generally best done with someone of the same gender. The optimal position is one that as closely reproduces an infant in arms as is possible with an adult-sized body, that is: both parties seated with plenty of pillows for support, and the person being held positioned heart to heart with the person doing the holding. It's particularly important to wholly support the head of the person who is "in arms," so he or she can relax into being held. The holding is done with little or no talking and lasts for fifteen to twenty minutes, sometimes more. With a little experience, the person being held will develop a sense of when they're "done," although a minimum of fifteen minutes is recommended. This process does not involve any fancy technology, just for the person holding to be attentive and present for the person being held; and for the person being held to relax and take in the loving touch. To take in the tangible expression of acceptance that comes with the simple act of lying in the arms of a friend can reorder our cells. Fear and negativity recede and a sense of wellbeing fills the body.

Parents will be familiar with the position and mood of holding because this is what we do with our child from day one. To give or receive formal holding as an adult can strengthen the objective mother or father within us in a way that feeds back positively into our parenting. Because I had regular holdings with women friends when my children were young, I became more aware of what holding can be for my growing child who is no longer "in-arms." When my eleven-year-old son wants to cuddle, I make sure to come to attention and take the opportunity to hold him with loving acceptance. Who doesn't need that?

Holding seems particularly valuable for women because it softens us, whereas the unique stress of our modern world tends to harden us. That hardness does not serve in the role of mother. Instead, the mood of soft strength produced in holding is exactly what is required to parent consciously.

HELP
The 6th Basic

In the journey of life we all need help. At no time is that more evident than during the parenting years. We need the good company and wise counsel of other parents and close friends as well as other reliable adults (aside from mother and father) to spend time with our children. More to the point, we need help navigating around (or through) the obstacles we encounter in ourselves when we take on the sacred task of parenting. A parent who is not receiving help with the purification of his character is dead in the water. Without this kind of help, we will parent our children as we were parented. The conscious parent recognizes the necessity to go beyond his "parenting program" in order to relate to life and childraising unhindered by the kinks of his individual psychology.

When she was First Lady, Hillary Clinton was fond of reminding us that "it takes a village" to raise a child. Unfortunately, in this day and age, most children are not raised in a village. Instead, children are raised in isolated single-family homes by a mother overtaxed by the sheer enormity of the job. I know well the trap we set for ourselves by thinking we would be better parents *if only* we had the right circumstances – in this case, a village at our disposal to assist us with the hard work of mothering. Still, there is definite validity to this idea of a having a community of support for parents.

Getting practical help with the job of parenting is one of the best gifts we can give both our children and ourselves. The notion that we can or should single-handedly shoulder the task of raising a child is an erroneous one. It feeds into our Western stance of stubborn independence, that "I'll-be-damned-if-I'll-ask-anybody-for-help attitude" we are famous for, and lends credulity to the mother-as-superwoman stereotype that many women are raised on.

On the other hand, putting our children in daycare before they are weaned from the breast or out of diapers is not the kind of help that takes a child's needs into consideration. Instead, taking that avenue can be symptomatic or supportive of the same attitude of stubborn independence mentioned above. Single working mothers with young children typically spend a large percentage of their earned income on childcare *so that they can work*. It's a kind of vicious cycle that makes no provision for home and family and is ignorant of the sacred role of mother to child. Another scenario is the stay-at-home mother who is going bonkers with her young children's demands and her lack of adult company all day long. She decides out of sheer desperation to go out to work because she can't take it anymore. Both women are suffering the lack of a village in helping to raise their children. In both scenarios the highest price is exacted from the child or children at the effect of the circumstance. Whatever our situation, we *can* compensate for the lack of a village in both large and small ways. If we can seek help, it will be of mutual benefit to our children and to us.

The Care of Our Children

When our children are babies, we do well to allow them to form relationships with other adults, first and foremost with their fathers. It is perhaps most natural for extended family and close friends of the parents to take on the role of "village" for a child. Aside from father, any caregiver for a young child should ideally make a long-term commitment to the care of that child and be a consistent presence in that child's life – one that he can count on, and build relationship to. The criterion for choosing caregivers is their ability to give a child of any age the proper respect and attention he or she is due.

The older a child is, the more time they can spend in the care of others besides their mother and father. In infancy it is wise to only leave a child in the care of someone who knows how to look after babies and whose parenting style is harmonious with our own. As a child grows we may look for caregivers who have specific skills or interests to teach our child that match her own inclinations.

Time Away from Our Children

If as parents we subscribe to the idea that we are the "be-all and end-all" of our child's existence, then indeed we may find ourselves with that burden – and no doubt all the sorrier for having to carry it. The more we can receive help with the raising of our children from those who are worthy of that trust, the better off we all will be. A wise counselor often pointed out to me that even the best of friends and the most happily married people need a break from one another sometime. He said that by way of supporting me in taking a " break" from my child. What we as mothers and fathers are looking for is time to renew ourselves away from our children while they are in the care of a responsible adult whose company is enjoyable and beneficial to them. That makes it a win-win situation.

With my first child I fell into this "be-all and end-all" syndrome. That approach was a combination of ignorance (not knowing how best to serve the particular needs of my son) and self-importance on my part. It *didn't* serve my child to be his exclusive adult relationship, but it unconsciously served *my need* to be needed. When my second child came along I had garnered sufficient experience with what didn't work with my first (fostering over-dependence on me), and enough insight into my own neurotic tendencies (the need to be needed), to make some better choices for my family and myself.

Time With Our Children

Of equal importance is for parents to spend *enough* time with their children. Although I have observed the tendency among parents practicing "attachment style" childraising* to be overly intent on their children, I would

---

* This term was conceived by pediatrician William Sears, and his wife Martha, to describe a highly responsive, attentive style of caring for a child. Attachment parenting promotes physical and emotional closeness between parent and child through what the Sears refer to as the "Baby Bs": bonding, breastfeeding, babywearing, bedsharing and boundary building.

guess that more parents spend too little time with their kids. There is great value in learning to heed our instinctive sense of how and when to take time away from our child or children. When I care to pay attention, I generally know, on any given occasion, if it's the right time to leave my kids, or if it would be better for all of us if I stay (assuming one has a choice.) Managing the ebb and flow of time together and time apart requires some skill and sensitivity on the part of parents. In general, the younger the child, the higher the ratio of time spent with the child ought to be.

A Sympathetic Ear

The daily demands of parenting call forth our deepest reserves of personal strength while at the same time often isolating us from contact with other adults. So, at a time when we most need to show up, we may be most on our own. This is not necessarily a bad situation, but it can be a challenging one.

Parents need the support and feedback of loving friends. Often a mother or father just needs someone to listen, a sympathetic ear. In the speaking of the "problem" and the receptive listening of the friend, something can be healed or clarified. When we hear our own words through a friend's kind listening, our own objective sense of the "solution" may emerge. For a mother to have another woman, or group of women, to talk to and spend time with on a regular basis is a wonderful and necessary thing; likewise for men.

The greatest gift we can receive from the good company of a real friend is support in accepting ourselves. When on our worst day, we can look into the eyes of a friend (or friends) who is listening to our story and see love and acceptance, that can be truly life-changing. The kind of support that accepts without needing to advise reinforces our own sense that we are capable of the task at hand. That can get us through the next day or even the next week!

When we become parents, we don't automatically know how to fill the shoes of mother or father that we find ourselves wearing. Other men and women can help us find the clarity and vision with which to fulfill that important responsibility. One thing I have noticed over the years is that a "day from hell" can show up when we least expect it. When children are under two, trying days can almost be planned on. All we can do is give our best in the midst of the struggle, realize it isn't like this everyday; and look forward to a new day which will generally bring a change in the emotional weather report. When the day of struggle is done, I usually reflect on the nature of the difficulties and my part in them. Regular or predictable struggles with our children generally call for some new approach to the problem. In such instances our own reflection on the situation may not be enough. Perhaps the problem necessitates a discussion with our husband or wife for further clarification. Our partners do see us more clearly than almost anyone else. We may call on that sympathetic friend's ear. It's also not uncommon to need outside feedback from a professional.

Feedback

Everyone needs help as a parent, even relatively whole and healthy individuals. It can be truly difficult to allow others to reflect us to ourselves, but the potential boon we receive from outside feedback is worth the trouble. Along the way in this long process that is raising a child, direct feedback whether from friends and family or a professional may be called for.

While receiving feedback can be hard, without it our effectiveness as parents will suffer. If we are able to hear how others perceive us, the insight can be priceless. To break out of negative inherited patterns of parenting we must make some significant effort, and taking feedback is key. If we *could* see ourselves clearly we probably wouldn't rely on the habitually problematic behaviors that we all have. When we do see ourselves with relative clarity in our more difficult moments in relationship, we generally do not see other options for how to be in the situation. We are "stuck in a rut." Others can reflect to us our unconscious behavior patterns, or ruts, as well as assist us in the process of developing new and better parenting skills. Seeking feedback at regular intervals, whether that means seeing a psychotherapist or family counselor, or just asking for help from a wise friend, is one more way to fuel the intention to make ongoing positive change in our parenting and in our lives.

Feedback from Our Children

Some of our best feedback comes from our children. They are, after all, intimately familiar with how we show up as parents and people. The innocent remark of a child can cut right to the heart of the matter. We commonly talk about the necessity to teach our children, but it's not always said that our children teach us as much or more than we teach them. In the grand scheme of things, it could be said that our kids are custom-fitted to teach us precisely the life lessons we most need to learn.

Children have no hidden agendas when they address us; they are just stating the obvious. If a child offers us feedback, we should be truly grateful to him or her for having the courage to speak up and say what they are thinking. If we are willing to listen and consider what is said, then we open the door for our child to develop the habit of being honest with us. As conscious parents we make a commitment to self-observe. If we are open, there is much we will perceive about ourselves with no outside help. But typically we also need the clues we receive when someone tells us about ourselves.

With our children, such feedback often comes in the heat of conflict and not when everyone is calmly sitting around the dinner table discussing the day. That requires us to have some humility with our kids. If we are intent on being "right" because we're the grown-ups, having the tables turned on us by our child can feel like a real loss of face. In reality, being able to take feedback from our children is a sign of our strength and wisdom as a parent.

Kids do say the darndest things. It's even pre-verbal. When my son was still small I remember trying to apologize for some foible of mine that he had been at the effect of. He reached up and covered up my mouth. My son's action said in effect, "Hey, mom, I know you're not perfect. So you messed up. That was then and this is now. Let's go do something else." He wasn't buying into my "bad mother" trip.

Over the years my children have made many priceless and revealing remarks to me. I've been stopped mid-nag by three words uttered by an observant child ("What's *your* problem?"); had my double-standards called ("You *always* let *her* get away with that."); my tone of voice challenged ("I won't do it if you talk to me like *that!*"); and my vanity skewered ("Mom, you always look *worse* after you fix your hair"). Although I don't always appreciate the feedback, I do consider what my kids say to me and attempt to use such remarks as honestly and constructively as I can, for all of us.

It *is* true that I sometimes take out a grouchy mood on my kids. I *do* tend to let my younger child get away with more than my older child. There *are* times when I unconsciously speak to my children in a tone of voice that is disrespectful and offensive. *I* think my hair looks better when I finish fixing it than when I started, but I *do* think I fuss over it too much and maybe that's what my kids really object to. *They* know that I am okay no matter what my hair looks like and they wonder if I know it.

And I have also said to my children, "You know, I didn't start feeling grouchy until you started fussing over (fill in the blank)." Or, "Your sister is younger than you and I don't expect her to be able to (fill in the blank) like you can." Or, "But you are using the same tone of voice with me! Did you notice that?" Or, "It really hurts my feelings when you say I look worse after fixing my hair." I only say those things to my children if they are true for me. I recognize the impulse to immediately give my child feedback as a way of deflecting what he or she is saying to me. Sometimes an interaction is brought to an abrupt close by my child's candor and I simply acknowledge my mistake and apologize.

My children not only tell me my hair looks bad, but also that my breath stinks, my cooking tastes awful, my outfit is ugly and they liked the living-room better *before* I rearranged it. Typically my response to such pronouncements is to laugh, most often because they are right. But sometimes my humor is aroused because their passionate conviction that they are right is really very funny. It's a guileless version of our own egocentric worldview. From such a perspective, my son doesn't see that his hair looks better before he combs it down flat before leaving for school. My daughter doesn't realize that her breath stinks in the morning too. They both get very attached to clothing I'd like to hide or burn, and neither of them ever seems to register that after I fix their food totally plain, like they ordered it, they often end up eating all of mine with the "icky stuff" (spices, onions, etc.) in it. When I help my children rearrange their bedrooms, they don't notice that the way they want things positioned isn't necessarily the best or only way to do it. All of this can serve as a ruthless and humorous reflection of that human quality of ours called "self-reference" or "egocentrism," whereby we are the center of the universe and our way is the only (and best!) way. About that, we can aspire to gently teach our children, and be scrupulously honest with ourselves.

Filling in the Blanks

Most of us will come to our parenting with an incomplete program. The job specifications include the struggle to fill in the blanks. Filling in the blanks can mean finding someone to guide our child along a stretch of the childhood path that we ourselves are unable to navigate properly with them. For instance, a friend of mine opted to have her daughter fully immunized but dreaded going with her to the doctor for the shots. Although this mother was certain of her decision, she found it personally upsetting to watch her daughter get shots and that compromised her ability to support her daughter through the experience. Her solution was to have an older woman friend, an experienced mother herself who had confidently had her own kids immunized, go with her child for the shots. Whether we believe in immunization or not, we've got to recognize the wisdom of someone who knows her own shortcomings.

Often, "filling in the blanks" can mean patterning off someone who has the skills we lack. This can be done by watching that person, either with our child or another, animate the quality we are missing. Maybe the person we pattern off is our child's teacher. We observe her work with our child's class and glean something we can use. We may ask for feedback from someone who sees us regularly with our child and can speak to the areas of difficulty. We may read a book and have a valuable insight sparked by the information it contains.

The heart of the work of "filling in the blanks" is finding the place within us that knows what to do but from which we are cut off. Until we have gained some familiarity with our kinks we won't necessarily be able to trust our own assessment of what is happening when we are handling a situation with our child poorly. That is why there is a need for outside input. We won't necessarily want to swallow, unexamined, every piece of feedback we receive either. The task of filling in the blanks involves developing discrimination about ourselves and others. A valuable place to begin is to learn to recognize, through experience, when we are in a "blank" area of our parenting.

A wise school administrator once remarked that, the way he saw it, teachers are going to make mistakes because they are human. The best we can hope for, he opined, is for a teacher to know when that has happened and to do whatever is needed to rectify the situation. Well, the same is certainly true of parents. We each have within us the capacity to parent well and to parent poorly and we can be sure we will experience some of both. Nearly any situation is workable with a child, even our mistakes, if we can be honest and loving despite our failures. Gaining self-acceptance and workability is the name of the game.

By the mercy of God and the generosity of my children, I am a more relaxed and wiser mother today. The process of filling in the blanks can happen for the conscious parent whether she actively seeks it or not, but the work is definitely facilitated by our willingness to accept help.

HELPING OUR CHILDREN

The relationship of parent to child is by definition one of helping our child along in the grand and glorious process of growing up. But what kind of help is most useful to them? How do we know when to hold their hand every bit of the way and when to step back and let them go? How much do we teach them about life and how much do we allow life to be the teacher? Some of these questions are addressed elsewhere in this book (see Chapter 3, about *Boundaries* and Chapter 10, *Holding On/Letting Go*). Here we will take a slightly different focus on how we can best help our kids.

A conscious parent must develop the presence to be there for her child when that is needed, the strength to step back or let go at the right times, and the wisdom to know the difference. At first our job is to help by being present, essentially. We nurse them, hold them, respond to their cries, bathe them and change their dirty diapers. When they begin to walk we hold their hands, steady their steps, and carry them when they are tired. We feed them their first solid food, keep them out of harm's way, and teach them their first words. That's big work for them and us! A child's need for that kind of help ought to be self-evident. The obviousness of it can make it easier to provide than the kind of help that requires us to teach and/or allow our children to progressively develop their independence from us.

Parent as Teacher

Not only do parents provide a child his or her first role model but they are also a child's first teachers. Parents "teach" a child about love by the way they hold and feed him or her in infancy. Parents guide a child through lessons in the laws of physics when he or she begins to toddle. And a parent is there to facilitate a child's growth into relationship with siblings, friends and other adults when he or she enters the more social preschool and school age years. Parents give a child their first boundaries. They foster both attachment (holding on) as well as separation (letting go) in their child.

Teaching from parent to child is not generally done in the form of long speeches. Kids usually prefer to get the message delivered in as few words as possible. Much of the teaching done by parents takes the form of helping their child deal with his head-on collisions with life and reality *as they occur*, as did the mother in the department store who wisely refused to give her daughter the toy she was demanding. At times we may teach by initiating a heart-to-heart talk that includes a gentle insertion of our adult wisdom about life and reality. Help and guidance are useful both in the moment when emotions are high, and later, when the heat is gone but the question and attendant feelings linger. We teach our children both by providing natural boundaries on their behavior, and offering them the truth in the form of an explanation about the nature of reality.

There is also the more mundane, but equally significant, level of teaching that occurs between mother or father and child. We teach our children how to tie their shoes, brush their teeth, ride a bike, cross the street, wash a dish, spell a word, understand a joke, write an essay, drive a car and so on. Such lessons are usually easy and straightforward. Along the way, of course, we get more of that oh-so-valuable on-the-job training in how to teach even the most ordinary things in the best way possible. Hopefully we as parents learn *our* lessons well and quickly.

Many of us may *not* have received valuable life wisdom from our parents. Even practical lessons may have been offered in a painful way, because our parents lacked the skills to teach pleasurably. That lack in itself can be an unfortunate lesson for a child in the nature of ignorance. In this way, a legacy of pain can be handed down from generation to generation. The best we can do with such an inheritance is to have compassion for its origins within our family, and strive to discontinue the transmission of this ignorance with our own children. If we manage that task we can be assured that we have taught our children well.

No Help

Sometimes, no help is help. Indeed, getting out of the way to allow kids to do their own learning can be hard for us. In our efforts to be good parents we may swing past the mid-point of balance and end up too far in the other direction. We find ourselves not only doing too much for our children but also allowing them to boss and sass us, as if they were spoiled royalty and we the live-in servants. As parents we must take care that we are truly preparing our children for adulthood by the way we interact with them and by what we teach and expect of them. A balance between over-control and no control is needed.

Offering no help can be an active or passive affair. Passively offering no help may involve purposely allowing a child to struggle to tie her own shoes when we could easily do it for her. Actively offering no help might entail gently refusing to tie the shoes of a child who is capable of doing that job for himself but won't do it, either out of habit, laziness or a lack of self-confidence. If we are the ones who habituated our children to having everything done for them, we must be especially skillful in teaching them to do for themselves. In this instance our child has been at the effect of our ignorance and is not to blame for living up to our expectation, or lack of it.

If a child is feeling lazy, we can model and teach a mature relationship to that most human of qualities. We might explain that it is possible and desirable to be able to act even when we don't feel like it. If there is a lack of self-confidence on the child's part, we can investigate what would allow him to become more confident. We might question ourselves about whether we are somehow creating or lending support to that weakness in our child by the way we are parenting him. Perhaps we have used a demeaning or impatient tone of voice when instructing or correcting our child. Or we may have the unexamined expectation that our child will fail.

Offering no help doesn't mean we neglect to teach a child the skills that are age-appropriate to them. Children do learn many things, probably the majority, by watching adults. But it can be a set-up for their failure and our disappointment to think they can learn all that they need to know that way. If we expect a child to make her bed or cook an egg, we will need to take the time to instruct her in what we know about the skill. We do best to keep our instruction short and to the point, and remain unattached to the results. A child may struggle mightily to do a simple job, or even opt to do it another way that works just as well but differs from our direction. Some skills may need to be taught many times before they stick. Children need the time and space to grow into their full capacity and potential, and we need the patience and fortitude to guide them lovingly toward that goal.

The Help of the Wisdom Teaching

Although I was raised in a Lutheran Protestant church in suburban New Jersey, I have spent my adult life in the study of the wisdom teachings of the spiritual traditions of the East. It is not that I have rejected my Western heritage, I have just been drawn more strongly to the traditions of the Orient. I am not a scholar of these teachings; instead, my study of them has been exclusively inspired and informed by my work with a living spiritual teacher. While it's certainly not necessary to have a spiritual teacher to be a conscious parent, in my own case my spiritual "apprenticeship," both to my teacher and to the teachings, has been irreplaceable in my parenting.

Because the spiritual teachings of all the traditions are concerned with the truth underlying all form, they cannot specifically help us with the practicalities of parenting. However, the teachings can lay the contextual foundation for our lives. As such, wisdom teaching is of the utmost relevance to the everyday job of parenting.

Mystical or wisdom teachings address the nature of reality and the eternal nature of the divine. Such teachings say this world and our lives within it are a kind of external show arising from the eternal ground of being. Our naturally fierce attachment to this life typically obstructs our having an objective relationship to living, and an accepting attitude toward dying. Wisdom teaching says it is possible to have our living be a preparation for our dying. To live with awareness of life's impermanence is to be genuinely detached from living. Then our lives are a demonstration of dispassionate action – action not invested in the outcome. Such action may also be called compassion or ruthless kindness.

Perhaps the idea of being detached from living sounds awful or only good as a way to buffer ourselves from the pain of life. But to live from this perspective would mean, among other things, freedom from the illusion that life revolves around us. Seeing clearly the larger picture, we could have an impartial sense of what was wanted and needed from us in any given moment. That kind of ability to discern the correct action and to render the appropriate service is at the heart of the sacred task of parenting.

Bringing new life into the world in the form of a child has much to teach us about exiting this life at death. Traffic in and traffic out. In the act of giving birth, we stand in the same doorway to receive new life as we pass through to leave this world. In *The Tibetan Book of Living and Dying* (HarperCollins, 1992), author Sogyal Rinpoche talks about the Buddhist idea of *bardos*. He says; "The word 'bardo' is commonly used to denote the intermediate state between death and rebirth, but in reality bardos *are occurring continuously throughout both life and death,* and are junctures when the possibility of liberation, or enlightenment, is heightened . . . The greatest and most charged of these moments, however, is the moment of death." (p. 11)

A bardo is a period or phase of darkness or descent, perhaps akin to the Christian idea of the "Dark Night of the Soul" – a journey of purification before entry into a higher understanding of the Divine. In my experience, there is a "parenting bardo" that represents the kind of opportunity Sogyal Rinpoche describes in the above quote. There is genuine love and joy to be experienced in our parenting, as in all of life. There is also hard work, deep sorrow and powerful negative emotions as well. This unexpected difficulty I call the parenting bardo. To confront our darkness, to make a descent to our unexplored depths, is not what we expected when we decorated the baby nursery in excited anticipation, but from the struggle is born the possibility for greater maturity and insight into our selves and our parenting. If we pass through the parenting bardo, we may emerge with the orientation to parenting that allows us to embrace it as the sacred task that it is.

Contrary to the impression made by the infant section of the local department store, full of soft blankets, toys that play lullabies and pastel baby suits, being a parent is likely to be more down and dirty than anything we've done before. When we're awake at 2:00 AM with a fussy baby, we come face to face with the state of our inner life. Some nights will be marked with anger and resentment over our lost sleep and the anticipation of a grumpy morning to follow. Other times, the body's fatigue will vanish in recognition of the joyous blessing we have been given in the form of the beautiful baby in our arms – fussy or not. Either way, if we are not steeped in the truth of existence, we are swimming alone in deep water without a life preserver. It's not enough to love our children. It's not even enough to be a good parent. We must have the capacity and the willingness to face ourselves, to "die" a little while we are still among the living. In his Foreword to *The Tibetan Book of Living and Dying* by Sogyal Rinpoche, the Dalai Lama says: "We cannot hope to die peacefully if our lives have been full of violence, or if our minds have mostly been agitated by emotions like anger, attachment, or fear. So if we wish to die well, we must learn how to live well: Hoping for a peaceful death, we must cultivate peace in our mind, and in our way of life." (p. ix)

Our attachment to our children may be the strongest earthly bond we ever have. To genuinely love and serve them, and then let them go, may be the hardest, most important thing we ever do. As parents we are in need of the wisdom teaching to be our compass as we navigate through the childraising years. The following are some truths specific to parenting that can be extrapolated from the wisdom teachings of the world's great religious traditions:

- Our children don't "belong" to us. We are merely their stewards. In truth, we possess nothing. We come from nothing and pass into nothing.
- We *will* pass on the legacy of our neuroses to our children because we are imperfect beings. Until we are honestly willing to face both our strengths and our weaknesses, real change cannot occur.
- The way we treat our children will affect who they become as adults and influence their long-term relationship to us. There is an operant law of karma whereby every action has an effect.
- Our children will grow up and leave home, if we've done our job right. All of life is a lesson in impermanence and the need for letting go.
- Trying to hide out with our shortcomings as a parent can have disastrous and sad effects. We all need help.
- It's not wise to believe everything we hear or read, but we shouldn't refuse the truth in whatever guise it appears.

Modeling the Wisdom Teachings

As a parent with religious values, I hope to pass on to my children something of my orientation to life. I want them to look beyond the surface level of appearances to discern the deeper truth of reality. I hope they will lead their lives with dignity and courage. It's important to me that they are growing up in an environment that includes a relationship to the Divine. We often discuss spiritual practicalities like the value of working to get along with others, of being willing to admit when we're wrong, or of having tolerance for one another's differences, and so on. I sometimes tell them how I came to study Eastern spiritual teachings and why I have a spiritual teacher. The thing I don't want to do is to form my children in my image.

My daughter was in pre-school with a girl whose parents observed a very restrictive diet. This little girl was made to follow that same diet. She was constantly an exception in school because she didn't eat what everyone else did. Fortunately for her, the school was very accommodating of her special needs, as set up by her parents. On one occasion, at a birthday party at one of the children's houses, I saw this little girl crying because she was not allowed to eat the candy that every other child there was eating. I took exception to her parent's lack of flexibility on this issue. Although their discipline in eating a very pure diet was commendable, every day their young daughter was singled out as different from everyone else because of that diet. They were laying a trip on their daughter in the name of their ideals.

The task of conscious parents is to raise children as free from their rigidity and hang-ups as possible, whether that rigidity involves candy or God. The best way to teach our religious values is to be a living example of them. That means we don't shy away from giving our children an education in our religious orientation, but we strive to be unattached to our children's life choices in this domain.

HUMOR
The 7th Basic

Without a sense of humor, life can be pretty grim. We are forever on the defensive against real or imagined attacks to our fragile sense of self-worth. When humor is not present, then we are buying the illusion that we have something to protect and defend. When we relate to the world that way, nearly everything is offensive or frightening. Thus the need to armor ourselves and be prepared to defend, or better yet to attack.

Years ago, before we had children (was there life before children?), my husband and I were both working for the same small business. One day we were having a fight. It was more like a cold war, actually, because we were both completely closed to resolving the argument and making sure to let one another know that the war was definitely still on. The fight didn't turn out as expected, however. Suddenly, magically, we caught one another's eye and saw through the pretense that there was something to fight about that was more important than the fact that we deeply and eternally loved one another. Immediately, we both started to laugh. It was all so absurd. What a relief! We could each stop pretending we had to go on nursing hurt feelings until the proper retribution had been made. From that perspective our conflicts were all so heavy and with no real resolution possible. What a gift to have humor arise. We have had many more fights since then but I have never forgotten that magical occasion when humor showed up like a life raft for the drowning.

To a child, the world is so new and big, overwhelming even, with its bewildering array of sights, sounds and experiences. As we guide our children through it, what better tool to have than a well-developed sense of humor – one that includes the ability to have humor about oneself! (Oh, no! Not that!) Yes, to have a well-developed sense of humor we do indeed have to be able to laugh at ourselves along with everyone else – maybe even the loudest and most genuinely.

A sense of humor about oneself (well developed, of course), allows us to have flexibility about the chaos that tends to show up around children. If we are in touch with our sense of humor then we are sure to be more relaxed than we would be without it. By disposition some people are more at ease with chaos and confusion, and others less so. I fall into the "less so" category. I love order and serenity, peace and quiet. You can imagine how the exuberance of two growing children has worked on me!

One practical skill I have learned is to put things in the order of their importance. In this way I can prioritize the never-ending list of things to do. To prioritize in action, we must be able to stop in the middle of one thing, just drop it, and go do the thing of greater importance. Attachment to the unfinished things must be released. Not that we never finish anything. It is possible to keep an inventory of all the balls we are juggling, deciding which ones to keep in the air and which ones to catch, and when. As I was writing this book, on some days the dishes sat dirty in the sink and the beds went unmade. On an ordinary day, if I plan to get my children to bed before midnight, I may need to leave the wash unhung and a conversation with my husband incomplete.

A sense of humor (well-developed, of course) allows us to recognize the ever-present nature of dishes, wash, unmade beds, bills and unanswered phone calls, and to know that they'll still be there when we're done tending our child. Of course we do need to work *against* chaos or it can engulf us. If we *never* get around to washing that stinking mound of dishes, we may need to look at our system of assigning importance. Either that or hire a house-keeper.

A sense of humor along with a big dose of relaxation will stand us in good stead at those times when we are awakened in the night from a dead sleep by our hungry, crying, restless or sick child. Humor and experience will give us the perspective to remember that all things pass, and that includes both our disrupted night of sleep and the childhood of our infant. And childhood ends more quickly than we can imagine in the moment! If we are relaxed and humor-filled enough, we might even savor those late-night wake-ups for the intimacy of time with our child when the rest of the world is asleep.

Laughter

Laughter is naturally infectious. When a roomful of people are all laughing, it's pretty hard not to join in. If we will allow ourselves to be humored by others or see the humor in everyday situations, the laughter that ensues can change a bad day to good in the moment of its graceful arising.

Our suffering is often quite humorous. When one child is crying, the other one complaining, your husband comes home from work cranky and tired, and you really need a break, what can you do? Laugh. Tell a joke, notice the humor in the horror of it all, tickle your complaining child, make a silly face. After all, if humor doesn't show up spontaneously, it's worth while faking it 'till it does. The arising of genuine humor in our worse moments only happens when we are truly seeing the situation for what it is and choosing not to go down with the ship.

It's also true that what's seems funny can be very situational. I've gone to movies that I know are funny but I did not laugh even once. It just wasn't funny that night. Contrary to my example above, I *have* sat in a roomful of people and not laughed even though everyone else was. The laughter of the group can seem stupid or even ominous when we are not partaking. Conversely, when I am full of humor I'll take any excuse to laugh. Everything is funny.

Children and Laughter

Although laughter with our children is a marvelous thing, it is important that kids know that laughter is not *at* them. There is a brand of humor that adults may indulge, intentionally or not, that is at the expense of children — usually making fun of their helplessness or innocence. Laughter of this sort must be seen for what it is and nipped in the bud. First and foremost we must track it in ourselves, and secondarily in others. Personally, we may reflect on our motive for taking advantage (through humor) of someone weaker than us, or dependent on us. With others (depending on the age of the child and the circumstances) we could either ignore the action, remove the child, or in extreme situations have the perpetrator leave. Sometimes we can just quietly speak to our child about what's going on while it's happening. Or we may be able to simply ask the adult, right in the moment, to stop the unacceptable behavior and explain why. If we can resolve such a situation without extreme measures, that is most desirable.

People are often saying the most well-intentioned and truly horrid things to children on the check-out line at the grocery store like: "My, aren't you a nice fat baby," or "Gee, I'd like to take you home with me. Do you think Mommy would be willing to part with you?" or "And how much does this baby cost?" When I was a new mother, I felt outraged and offended by such comments. With the passage of time and the accumulation of experience, now I usually just laugh and make a good-humored response: "Oh, this baby is definitely not for sale!" Such a remark makes the necessary communication to all concerned.

Play

Having a child or children in our life is a wonderful opportunity to re-learn the fine art of play. Being with children can give us an innocent connection to life that we may have forgotten. Playing a game of peek-a-boo with our toddler, making "music" on overturned pots and a toy piano, or creating a work of art from construction paper and glue with our older child, can be sheer pleasure. When we really enter into the spirit of play or creative expression with our children, we experience the humming of a happy heart. Such an experience can be like water in the desert for us serious adults.

Play is the outward expression of good humor and a mood with many forms. Play may show up as kissing the baby's feet, blowing on his soft round belly, or dancing with him when he's cranky or restless, just for the sheer joy of it. Babies do like to be danced.

At a certain age, "Tell me a story" becomes a chant for many little ones. The first time a child ever asked me to tell a story was when I was in my twenties and had no children of my own. The look of innocent expectation on that child's face was lost on me. I was struck dumb. The thought of *making up* a story and then speaking it aloud was terrifying. I don't remember if I ever told a story to that child. Surely I must have tried because I saw her often and she persisted in asking me that question nearly every time.

With my own children I have, of course, passed many the hour telling imaginary stories. We've even told stories in installments or chapters. Most of those stories are completely forgotten now, they have disappeared into the mist of our memories. But they were marvelously alive at the time.

I have often had great difficulty or resistance to playing the game of "Tell me a story." I have to be ready to step into that childhood place of playfulness and magic. When I'm grouchy it's hard to be playful. Really hard. On occasion I have successfully pushed through the inertia to enter the land of play. At other times I have not been able or willing.

I enjoy playing with my children. I once read an article in a parenting magazine that claimed that the average parent spends very little time playing with their child. The author recommended taking at least fifteen minutes each day to play with our kids. Hmm. Fifteen minutes. When I read that article I realized that I was way over my daily quota. Still, it's not a bad guideline. Not everyone has the choice to be a stay-at-home parent. My husband and I have been willing to manage on one income, in order to have a full-time parental presence (me) for our children.

I did play too much with my first child. It's good to make the distinction between parent and playmate. A parent is not a playmate. Moms and dads do play, but should not be expected to be a full-time entertainment service! Children ought to be encouraged to learn to occupy themselves. In the right dosage, "alone time" builds their skills of imagination and an appreciation of solitary activity. To enter into the spirit of play with our children we do not need to actually get right down there and play with them. It's great to be able to do that, important to do that, yet the mood of play can take the form of allowing and appreciating our child's play. If we understand that a child's play is also their work, a crucial facet of the incredible process of their growth and evolution to adulthood, then we will be respectful and encouraging of it even if we do not always participate in that play. For example, a young child can be completely engaged taking shells, stones, or wooden beads out of a basket, and then putting them back in.

Joseph Chilton Pearce, in his book *The Magical Child,* recommends that we never disturb the reverie of a child. If we are practicing sensitivity to our children then we will notice when they are working or otherwise occupied, and respect their activity.

The joy of playing with my kids is something I will definitely miss when they have grown. Hopefully my children and I will be friends and will "play" together as adults.

RESPECT
The 8th Basic

Advocating For Our Children

For the conscious parent, advocacy means taking a stand for our children's essential goodness and right to be treated with respect, as well as protecting their innocence. For many of us, it's likely that no one advocated for us as children, and we'll need to get over the unfairness and the hurt of that in order to advocate for our own children. Realistically it may take years to really heal that wound. In the meanwhile, our child still needs us to act as an advocate even if we must wrestle with our own feelings to do so. That's doing the right thing.

Conscious parents also advocate for their children in the company of others. Well-meaning family members, friends and even strangers may unknowingly do and say things to and about our children that are disrespectful of them. It is sometimes necessary to ask someone who is treating our child disrespectfully to stop or change their behavior, even though they may not understand or agree with our perspective. The use of pet names (often demeaning to the child); talk about how a child has "his father's nose" (when in reality he has *his own* nose); or remarks about the smell of a child's full diaper, are examples of potentially disrespectful behaviors. For adults who unconsciously mock children due to ignorance, or to mask their own deep-seated childhood hurt, this can be very difficult behavior to change.

With strangers or anyone who will not have a lot of contact with our child, it is generally best not to say anything to them directly, but instead to discreetly explain the truth of the situation to our child. We ought to take a stand for our children, and even be hard-line about it at times. But it's equally important to relax and remember to have a sense of humor. That will serve our children most of all, because how *we* relate to the world around us is what impacts *them* most. Humor and relaxation are two basic ingredients for conscious parenting. We're not going be able to advocate for our child without them. Having a standard for child advocacy and respectful relationship with children makes it possible to parent with dignity and consciousness. But without humor and relaxation, we will be rigid and unhappy doing what should be an essentially joyous job – raising our children.

How to Respect Our Children

Conscious parents show respect for their children by being responsive to them from birth. To be respectful is to refrain from talking about children when they are present – even if they are sleeping. That means not telling stories to others, in front of our child, about something he did that was cute or embarrassing, or even amazing. That's a courtesy most of us know how to extend to other adults, but do not generally extend to babies and children. Likewise we respect our children by not using excessive "baby talk" with them as if they were life-size dolls; instead we recognize that a loving normal voice is generally best.

When conscious parents speak of their children, they take care to do so with respect and regard. That leaves out complaining and making fun of children, or acting like there is some "problem" with or about them. In infancy especially, children should be fed when they are hungry, and held when they cry. A baby's cry is her main way of communicating. We refrain from suppressing her cry, while being attentive and responsive to the meaning of that cry.

Respectful Listening

As they grow, respect for children extends to listening when they are speaking to us. We may find that we have a different standard of manners for adults than we do for kids. Oftentimes we miss our child's attempts to communicate to us because we have "tuned them out." As such, we may notice particular times to be on alert to our children. As a parent who aspires to be conscious, I recognize that I must not allow anyone to so dominate my attention that I am unavailable to my children. Therefore, I must be especially attentive to pick up my children's cues when I am involved in a compelling conversation with an adult.

Another time to be on alert is when kids are present in the midst of a gathering of adults. I have noticed the tendency of groups of adults to unintentionally ignore the children present. If we practice respectful attention to our children in such situations, we may find ourselves with a crowd of interested kids around us – all the children present at the gathering! Children are generally quite pleased to have the genuine attention of an adult (for many children it's a novel situation), and they make truly delightful company themselves. Paying respectful attention to our children doesn't mean we should, or even could, be perfectly attentive at all times. What is important is that we not let them get lost in the shuffle of our busy adult lives.

Recently, on the playground at my children's school, I watched a little girl of three or four repeatedly tug on her mother's arm to get her mom to watch her pull herself up between two picnic tables. The mother was busy talking with her older son about his lunch. (Children do have the vexing habit of trying to get our attention no matter what else we are already involved in.) As I watched, this little girl said the same thing over and over to her mother, her voice taking on a mechanical quality, as she got no response to her repetitive call. This mother had tuned her child out. Every parent has been guilty of this at one time or another. It's absolutely crucial to be clear with kids about when and how our attention is available. And, if we cannot give them our attention when they are asking for it, we should take a moment to tell them that, and then be sure to give them our attention when it *is* free. That's treating children with the respect they are due.

Respecting Children's Property

Sometime in the toddler years, children begin to understand the concept of "mine." This usually shows up as possessive behavior over favorite toys. When my son was this age, I eagerly made one of his first play dates with the child of a friend of mine. We mothers were happily anticipating a pleasant afternoon of good company. What happened instead was that my son, passionately and tearfully, refused to allow her child to touch even one of his toys. The play date ended abruptly after it began. I felt disappointed, upset and embarrassed. Plans had been dashed, the other little boy traumatized, and my own child's behavior was selfish and unkind, or so it seemed. What I didn't know at the time is that the outcome of this arrangement was as predictable as clockwork. Children this age don't understand the concept of sharing because they are busy with "mine."

Beginning with the toddler's toys, as children grow, they acquire property. Although we may have purchased every one of our kid's possessions, they are nonetheless their property. Parents ought to respect children's possessions as we would anyone else's. In toddlerhood, we may be firm that our child will need to share some toys with visitors, but allow them to choose which ones, and to put away the ones he or she feels most attached to before the company arrives. Likewise we wouldn't throw away or alter something of our child's without their permission. Although I have to admit to surreptitious room cleanings when the sheer volume of stuff in my kids' rooms threatens to bury us all, I never get rid of anything I think my child would be attached to keeping. Generally I throw away a certain category of things like school papers and old drawings, and carefully make piles of other items to be reviewed and decided on by my child. Now that my son is approaching his teen years, I don't go through his stuff without his okay.

Both of my children have asked their father and I to knock before entering their rooms. At first, that was hard to remember to do, but it also gave us the opportunity to ask our kids to give us the same courtesy. The idea is that we treat children as equals as much as possible, even while maintaining our role as parents (an important qualifier). When we role model respect for our children, we make a more powerful communication than all the preaching in the world could likewise effect.

Children's Appearance

Respect for children also extends to not making undue comment on their physical appearance. This can be a difficult impulse for a parent to control, but we must recognize that a child is a work in progress. Throughout their early years, children need the space to grow and change through all the stages leading to who they will be as an adult. In our role as guardians we should have the implicit understanding that appearance is not the definition of a child's emerging identity.

None of us chooses our physical appearance, we are born with it. We do choose our particular style. Style *is* a matter of personal taste. Our style makes a strong communication to ourselves and others, and the content of that communication is worth paying attention to. If, for instance, our child's personal style has become objectively offensive (note the qualifier "objective"), that is cause to make a boundary. But if we just can't bear the way our pre-teen has chosen to comb his hair, or we wish we could burn our eight-year-old's favorite pants because we're tired of looking at them, that's a difference of style. Unless we as parents are called upon to draw a needed boundary, excessive or inappropriate comment or concern over body size or shape, hair-style, clothing choice, or blemishes is disrespectful. Such comment draws superficial attention to appearance and has the potential to destroy the innocence of a child by making him self-conscious (subtly shamed) and/or overly concerned about how he looks.

Hygiene

Practicing good hygiene is a way of respecting ourselves and others. If a child's feet stink from wearing his sneakers barefoot, his hair needs washing, or he has smelly farts, a sensitive comment or kindly guidance may be needed (assuming the child is old enough to be responsible for his own hygiene.) Sensitive comment doesn't make a child feel somehow wrong for the fact that a body needs caring for. Kindly guidance lets him know that everybody's feet stink when confined inside shoes. Feet and shoes need washing. Hair does need to be shampooed on a regular basis, particularly as a child gets older and his oil glands become more active. Everybody experiences intestinal gas. Sometimes kids need a reminder to realize they need to use the toilet. Older children need instruction in when and where it's okay to "let it rip" and when to be more discreet with body sounds like farts and burps.

The Etiquette of Appearance

Educating our children about appropriate attire for various situations and places is beneficial. In this way we teach our children to have respect for their environment. For young children, there is a difference between clothing worn to the playground and clothing worn to church. For teens, clothing that might be worn to a rock concert is probably not what would be worn to school, and so on. In general, the younger the child, the wider the tolerance on suitable attire. When my children were young, I always figured getting where we were going in a relatively relaxed and timely fashion was more important than the kids looking perfectly groomed. Then too, as children get older they can better understand social convention with regard to clothing. Finally, in the pre-teen and teen years, it can be very important and valuable, when necessary, to take a strong stand on acceptable attire.

Draw No Conclusions

A natural extension of this principle of not placing undue attention on outer appearance, is taking care not to judge our children based on how clever, popular, or grown up they may or may not seem. Although it is natural to be concerned with our children's progress to maturity, conclusions about how they have turned out, based on appearances, are probably best left until after they have grown into adulthood.

With love and acceptance, each child will flower in his or her own time. It takes discipline for us parents to not burden a child with our fears, projections and expectations. Even too much praise can be burdensome for children. Any behavior of ours that puts artificial attention on kids is not a service to their natural growth and development, and disrespects their essential wholeness.

RELAXATION
The 9th Basic

A woman I admire, a mother, once said that what is required of the conscious parent is to not be uptight about *anything*. If one can be essentially relaxed as a parent, with all the sacrifices the job demands, then one will be in the correct posture to parent consciously and contentedly. The relaxation referred to here is *not* kicking back on the couch with a magazine and a box of chocolates. The relaxation that the conscious parent benefits from practicing is relaxation-in-action. Some people are naturally more disposed to this than others, but we can all build our stamina and ability with experience.

Relaxation-in-action requires a degree of self-knowledge that many of us do not have to begin with. Such self-knowledge means that we see ourselves with some clarity, and can face our emotions without needing to run away or hurt someone. To be able to practice relaxation-in-action is the beginning of acquiring the "peace in our mind" which the Dalai Lama has described.

Relaxation is relevant to all the large and small sacrifices we are called to make as parents. It's natural enough to feel stressed when the new baby prevents us from getting as much sleep as we need; or when our toddler disturbs every mealtime by mashing and throwing food and demanding to "get down." When our school-age child just won't get dressed and ready for school in a timely fashion, or our teenager is demanding to be driven to a friend's house, we may wonder just what we got ourselves into when we welcomed our little bundle of joy into the world. We only discover what the parenting job-specifications are when it's too late to change our mind about whether we really want the work.

The reality is that there are no "easy" children. But if we recognize the relatively short-term nature of our sacrifices and the value to our children when we can be truly responsive to their needs, we see that our gracious acceptance of what's required makes everyone happier. Of course we will have grumpy days, and times when we'll complain. That is only human. But an overall attitude of relaxation is an irreplaceable tool in this big job that is conscious parenting.

In hindsight I count my blessings that I've got kids in my life that will enter my comfort zone fearlessly and wreak havoc on my status quo. What I've learned from parenting my children has made me an infinitely better person than I was before I had kids.

Relaxation-in-action allows us to face the huge responsibility of caring for our children with humor and confidence. Watching the parents on the playground at the local park, it's clear who is a first-time parent and who has more

103

than one child. When normal playground events happen, like a scraped knee or an argument over a sand bucket, the over concern of the new mom or dad compounds the situation, while the laid-back style of the more seasoned parent generally allows for an easeful resolution of the difficulty.

One afternoon at the local playground I got to test my senior status as a mom. It was a day in late winter, still cool and damp, and there was no one else at the park. My daughter and her friend were squealing and running up and down the large colorful play structure. I was sitting off to the side daydreaming in the sun when the cries of my daughter broke through my reverie. Amazingly, she had wedged her plump toddler knees between the vertical plastic "bars" at one side of the upper level of the play structure, and now she was stuck. With her knees caught in this way, she could not quite put her feet down flat to support herself, thus adding to her discomfort. She was crying and panic-stricken.

"Can you just pull them out?" I inquired, feeling oddly calm.

"No!" came the tearfully definitive response. As her friend stood by watching curiously, I tried pushing my daughter's knees free from my side of the bars. They wouldn't budge. I had a sudden vision of firemen sawing through the bars to release her trapped knees. Wow, this could get complicated, I thought.

I glanced around the playground and the nearby neighborhood houses, but not a soul was in sight on this sunny quiet afternoon. I told the girls that I was going for help, and knocked at the door of the closest house, thinking I'd use the phone to call for whatever sort of assistance one needed in such situations. No one answered the door. On my way back past my car to the playground, I stopped. On a whim, I grabbed the small bottle of hand lotion I usually carry in my backpack. Reaching my still trapped daughter I proceeded to rub hand lotion all over and around her knees, and *voila!* first one knee and then the other popped free. After rubbing her sore knees for a moment, my daughter resumed her carefree play. I sat back down in the sun feeling grateful for such an easy resolution to what initially looked like a real problem. I was proud of myself for keeping my cool.

Many such unique moments occur in the life of a child. Having lived and panicked through a variety of them with my son, I like to think that because I remained calm this time, the idea to use hand lotion on my daughter's knees occurred naturally. A stroke of genius under stress.

Some people are just relaxed by nature. I know a young mother who is very spacious and wise with her two young children. I marvel over her easeful approach. I recall watching her calmly cooking in her kitchen with her young son in a back carrier. He was gleefully eating a piece of ripe banana and grabbing onto her shirt with his banana-laden little hands as well. Equal amounts of banana were going onto her shirt as were going into his mouth. She was unconcerned. I was impressed. I don't mean to suggest that every mother should have the same standard as she, but having a wide tolerance for chaos and disruption goes a long way with kids.

For the rest of us who are naturally uptight we can learn through our parenting experiences to recognize what is most important in the moment and what is less so. We may have to go against natural inclinations to respond appropriately. For instance, one of the hardest sacrifices for me is to leave dishes in the sink and beds unmade, because I like my house clean and neat. But when my child is sick, or everyone woke up late for school, I can practice "letting it be" because there is a higher priority than my desire for things to be tidy. We can trust that the messy house will get taken care of in its turn and remember that our children will only be young once.

It's not that one style of parenting is better than another. Each has something to offer the other. That naturally-relaxed mother may have to struggle to put an orderly house on her list of priorities at all. Chaos can threaten to consume her life. Growing up in a chaotic environment may as adversely affect her children as the actions of a mother who won't stop cleaning the kitchen to really listen to hers. Balance is the name of the game. The practice of relaxation-in-action is at a deeper level than disposition and learned habits. Essential relaxation springs from a place of wisdom and compassion.

Disarming Ourselves

Essential relaxation puts us into a posture of non-aggression in relationship to our world. I call this "disarmament." Disarming ourselves is giving up the defenses that armor the heart. That takes real courage. My children help me disarm, because although I can justify "the fight" with other adults, I know in my heart of hearts there can be no fight with a child. Children are free of malice.

I remember when I figured out as a youngster that I could "get" my older sister by having a nasty retort ready for her when she and I were fighting. It felt good to be able to defend myself against her. What became evident as I grew older was that the effect of my nastiness was not helpful in resolving differences with others. I saw that cutting words (especially the four-letter variety) only served to escalate the clash and heighten the mutual desire to be right at all costs. Although I had seen this effect, I cannot say I gave up the habit of "sticking it" to those around me when I thought they deserved it. It was actually just a knee-jerk defensive reaction: get them before they get you. And so I bumbled along through my twenties and into my thirties mostly just responding through habit, occasionally acting contrary to it. And then I had a child and came to see that my helpless babe was innocent of such adult motives, which left me face to face with only myself.

Sharp Edges

Children inadvertently step on our corns so easily and so often. They run roughshod over our hang-ups from day #1. Kids are generally guileless, their only real motive being to know that we, their parents, love them. And they do test the limits, strength and maturity of that love. They test us not to give us a hard time but just because they are growing up, and have to live and learn and be guided like all young creatures.

Our sharp edges show up in all the little ways we feel offended or annoyed by our children, and then lash out in some way. "Losing it" with our kids is obviously not the ideal scenario. But it can and will happen despite our best

107

intentions, and even if we've read all the books on how to do parenting "right."

Usually we feel threatened by things that trigger our insecurity, or our secret pain, or even just things that are annoying or insulting. It's up to us to sort out whether we have been triggered into historic hurt, or if we are responding in a healthy manner to unacceptable behavior toward us on the part of our child. Often it's both. No matter what is going on, the challenge is to stay present and make a suitable response. But here the key is not *what* we do; it's *how* we do it. The right words: *"I'm not appreciating your demanding tone of voice. I would like to be spoken to with respect. If you are unable to do that right now, please come back and talk to me when you can,"* are no good if they are said with the intention to jab. Kids seem to have unerring radar for even the merest hint of a "plugged in" tone on the part of grownups. They may cry or get angry when we are rightfully firm with them, but the difference between that response and the outrage children express when we mistreat them should be clear.

The emotional climate we create for our children with our overall approach to people and life, as well as the way we handle the difficult moments with them, will affect our children for a lifetime. That's a huge responsibility. The good news is that our kids are incredibly resilient and forgiving of us. As long as they see us making efforts toward parenting consciously, including admitting when we have made a mistake, they will generally give us a break.

"It's okay to make mistakes as long as you learn from them," a wise friend of mine recently remarked. I recognized the truth of those words, yet I've watched myself make the same mistakes all my life. One big difference now is that I know they are mistakes. I used to think everybody else was wrong. (Ah, the arrogance of youth!) The presence of children in my life provided me the urgency to begin on a long, slow learning-curve in relationship to my sharp edges. I am easily offended and quick to feel criticized; yes, even by a child. But my kids have helped me to get over myself. The call is to become on one hand more sensitive to how our behavior effects those closest to us, and on the other hand, more resilient in response to how others effect us. We develop a tough skin with a soft heart.

Ultimately, getting beyond our sharp edges to a disposition of essential relaxation is a feeling thing, not an "I've-got-it-figured-out" thing. Because there is no hard and fast recipe for how to handle every situation with a child, we must grow our sense of intuitive presence. This probably won't happen overnight. But gradually, time after time, if we go deeper into the call of the heart – ours and theirs – we can come to know how to respond to each new moment in the life of our children.

Minding our sharp edges doesn't mean we have no teeth in our parenting. Indeed, with the genuine softening of the heart (essential relaxation), we are able to see with greater clarity the need for and value of holding the line with our children. To be able to respond free of sharp edges means we have allowed our life and our loved ones to teach us about how we fall short. Then we've taken those lessons and learned further to embrace our humanity in its entirety. And in the full, embracing, acceptance of oneself, the sharp edges will soften.

Dealing with Anger and Resentment

I was shocked to feel the force of my anger toward my children when they were still just babies; horrified to find myself having such un-motherly feelings. In truth I was unprepared for the full range of emotions (including anger) that would arise as a mother. In hindsight I recognize that beneath the anger were feelings of helplessness and/or fear. I didn't know how to handle a defiant child or effectively set a boundary for a lively youngster. Naturally enough, angry feelings arose in response to my feelings of inadequacy. I never imagined a child could get my goat like this! And furthermore that I would be so at a loss for how to respond.

I always considered myself a calm and peaceful person before having children. In the domain of how to relate to my anger, I found myself missing a basic ingredient in the recipe called parenting.

What makes working with our angry or resentful feelings so challenging is that we must first learn to manage the fiery emotions before we can address either the needs of our child in the present moment, or our own underlying issues. Besides the emotions that flare up in the present moment, we may find ourselves triggered into the emotions of our own childhood experience at the same age. These "historic" emotions can overlay and color our perception of present reality. While we work on acquiring the parenting skills we do not have, we must also unravel the psychological kinks that bind up our ability to respond objectively. If that sounds like a big job, it is. If the parenting task overwhelms us, this is one of the key reasons why.

Although is it best to have an accepting attitude toward our less-than-appropriate emotional expressions when they arise, it ought to be obvious that unchecked anger on the part of a parent can be very destructive. This is perhaps the one emotion about which we have to be most mature. To walk the razor's edge of acknowledging healthy anger in ourselves and our kids without allowing the negative expression of this most potent of emotions requires genuine skillful means. In her book *Love and Anger, The Parental Dilemma* (Viking Penguin, 1991), Nancy Samalin says: "Our goal, then, is not to eliminate the feelings of anger from our parental repertoire. We couldn't even if we wanted to. Rather, it is to find ways to express ourselves when we are angry that do not hurt, insult, demean, or inspire revenge and rage in our children." (p. 16.)

For conscious parents to be able to work with anger constructively, we have to have wrestled with our primal emotions and come up with newfound acceptance and understanding of the human condition. While that might not seem like the most savory of pastimes to the personality, it is rigorously good work for the soul. And we have our children to thank for this most valuable opportunity. When we have confidence in our ability to navigate our own emotional "underworld," then we can embody relaxation-in-action with our children.

HOLDING ON
LETTING GO
The 10th Basic

Throughout this book we have talked about "holding on" as a means of nurturing our bond with our child and honoring our child's bond to us. To attach or bond with a child requires that we have the wisdom and maturity to give of ourselves utterly, all the while knowing that if we do the job right, our children naturally separate from us at the appropriate time. So much of early childhood requires that we hold onto our child. But throughout even those early years, letting go is intertwined with holding on. It's just that the holding on "practice" is such an all-consuming one. Yet at a certain point the predominance of holding on must give way to letting go.

THE FUNDAMENTALS OF HOLDING ON

The profoundly physical bond we share with our child begins during pregnancy. Mother's womb is a snug, dark room just the right size for a growing fetus. Nourishment flows into the infant's body through the umbilical cord, and the baby is gently rocked by mother's walking. The holding on happens organically, automatically at this stage. Mother's body knows how to do it and we can marvel at that. It is humbling.

Before birth, mother and father can build an emotional bond with their child by welcoming him into their hearts as he is materializing within mother's body. The emotional climate parents create for their growing child produces the chemistry in which their baby will be awash during pregnancy. We don't have to be perfect - never tired, grumpy or doubting. It's simply optimal to hold a consistent mood of acceptance and love toward the growing fetus. Both parents benefit from such an emotional posture toward the pregnancy, and the baby, too, profits because he or she profoundly shares mother's chemistry (emotional and actual) in utero and during the early in-arms stage of infancy.

Once a child has been birthed, the holding on is not so automatic. Although instinct tells us to keep our infant in-arms, we will have to buck the popular parenting theory that advises us to put our newborn on a feeding schedule, give her a crib in a separate room, and let her learn to cry it out so that she doesn't come to expect a prompt response to every cry. If we are able and willing to follow the body's intuition, we will keep our child in-arms, respond to her cry, and feed her when she's hungry.

Babies want to be held securely and lovingly, close to mother or father. Sometimes a new parent has to learn how to carry his or her child correctly. I'm guessing that if a person was not held much when he was an infant, holding his own child might not come naturally. Parents, especially

113

mother, are an infant's contact with earth, his or her con-nection to solid ground. A child held securely has got a sure connection both to mother *and* to earth. A baby held loosely or insecurely will instinctively fear falling from her mother's arms. Such a fall obviously represents physical danger to the body, but also a loss of contact with mother and ground.

Whether holding comes naturally to us or not, if we simply do it, the body will remember in time how to do it optimally. The more we hold our child, the more connect-ed or bonded to that child we will be. And when we are attuned to our infant in this way, we will notice how to hold our baby so that he or she is properly and comfort-ably supported.

As children grow into toddlerhood, holding on means allowing the flowering of children's exploratory quest, while keeping them safe from serious harm. We not only continue to hold our child in-arms as needed; we also hold them in the safety of the wider embrace of our attending presence. At this point in the development of a child, it's wise to kidproof at least one space in our home so we can relax somewhere. Otherwise, the questing toddler really does require almost constant attending.

Open arms are still crucial to the toddler even though he or she is not continually in-arms as during infancy. Frequent pit stops to nurse, or just to be held, refuel the busy toddler for the important work of exploring and learning about their world. Retreat to mother or father's arms is also in order for most toddlers when anything new or threatening appears.

Making A Home

One obvious yet essential way we hold our children is by giving them a home to grow up in. Having kids around will generally prompt our organic urge to provide a suitable and nurturing place in which to raise those kids. The presence of young children in our lives automatically anchors us in the home. For one thing, home is about the best place to be when children are young. Too many transitions and unfamiliar places in their daily round of activity tend to disturb young children.

Home is the place where a family eats, sleeps, works and plays. Thus, the home we make ought to be livable, yet elegant. The simplest way to do that is to keep our living spaces simply appointed and clean. We ought to have what we need, while keeping clutter to a minimum. Simplicity in our lifestyle and living place will automatically engender elegance.

Perhaps most importantly, home is the place where a family lives together in intimate relationship with one another. The extent to which we are available to our children, especially in the early years, will determine whether they feel held in their home and family. The degree to which we avoid or buffer ourselves from intimacy is what fosters isolation and disconnection between us and our kids. Children expect touch and love and intimacy. They want to connect with their world, and that means us.

The home we create ought to be a sanctuary, not a cage. Children should feel that home is where they can receive the respect and love they are due as they grow and stretch their wings. If we haven't stifled and disrespected them, they will come to us with their questions and concerns along the way to maturity. Conflicts will arise within any family. Yet if home becomes a battleground for a child, we can be sure something is amiss in our home-making.

Giving Kids a Childhood

Kids these days often have schedules as hectic and stressful as any adult's. After a long day of structured activities at school, children (and parents) should be able to go home and stay there. Childhood ought to include lots of unscheduled time where nothing *has* to be done. If my oldest child tells me he's bored, I think it's a healthy thing. He has enough of nothing to do. At age eleven, my son is having his first experience of an after-school activity. The fact that he has not played a sport or studied an instrument before now was his own choice and my unspoken preference. My son hasn't suffered the lack of lessons and practices. In general, he makes very good use of his unstructured time.

Most children and families today don't have the benefit of the old-fashioned neighborhood of days gone by, where kids could congregate in the street or on the sidewalk for companionship and games. For some reason, be it fear for children's safety, isolationism, or too much TV and computer time, people don't come out of their houses and mix it up. In order for kids to play together, locations, times and transportation have to be arranged. That can get to feeling like a pretty un-natural effort exerted to provide for a pretty normal need. There doesn't seem to be any way around it other than to seek out a neighborhood where people *do* come out of their houses (are there any?), or to create old-fashioned community to the best of our ability, with church members or school families.

All along the way in the raising of children, the holding on and the letting go are intertwined. They are two sides of the same coin. The bond we nurture with our holding on pulls our child close to us, literally and figuratively, but it also cues us to when we need to let go.

LETTING GO

Starting when our children take their first steps away from us as toddlers, letting go becomes a distinct counterpoint to our holding on. A toddler *wants* to exercise his independence from his parents. Children this age are often determined to do things for themselves. If we button up his jacket and tie his shoes, a toddler may unbutton and untie both, and then redo them for himself. This behavior can seem bothersome in the moment (I already dressed this kid!), but if we can see it for what it is – a healthy step towards independence – we'll want to encourage this movement in our child. The holding on of the in-arms stage of parenting is relatively straight forward. With toddlers, the holding on and the letting go happen rather simultaneously.

When our children reach school age (or thereabouts,) the tide really begins to turn from holding on to letting go. Clearly children want to affirm our holding on as they step into their letting go. When it came time for my daughter to begin the first grade, she needed me to help her make the adjustment to spending all day at school. With her teacher's consent, I stayed in the classroom right at my daughter's side (which was exactly where she wanted me)

117

in the first weeks of school. When she was ready, I moved off at a short distance to just observe and be "on call" when my daughter wanted me. When it became evident that my presence was no longer necessary, I didn't stay. No other child had anyone available to her in this way. Yet, without undue comparison to others, I found it valuable to do the right thing for my daughter. I was watchful for any inappropriate holding on, on my part, while trusting that her growing process would naturally take my daughter to the next step. In this case that was to stay at school without me. And she did.

As parents, we lead or guide our kids through the process of letting go. They do not have prior experience with moving through the steps to maturity. We are their security in the face of the unknown. It's natural enough they should cling to us. And yet, despite a child's lack of experience, they are truly bold adventurers at heart. The intrepid toddler is not only learning the precise skill of walking, but also beginning a grand quest to explore every inch of his world. That's an awesome double hurtle that he tackles fearlessly. It could be said that our job is to simply support that toddler spirit throughout his growing up; to encourage him to keep striking out boldly.

A mother I know whose lively daughter is a friend and schoolmate of my daughter shared with me this anecdote of her parenting experience. "I have been so painfully shy my entire life," she said "and have truly suffered that tendency in myself. I was determined that Sarah not be saddled with the same limitation. So I have consistently encouraged her to step out in all situations so as not to develop the habit of insecurity." And I can verify that her daughter is a fearless, strong and bright child. She is very much her own person, delightfully spirited and bold.

The failure to release our children at the right time has its roots in our own incomplete process of separation. As evidenced by Sarah's mom, it's not that we have to be perfect to support that process of separation or letting go in our child. What is needed is an honest familiarity with and acceptance of our own shortcomings, coupled with the willingness and ability to act against our limitations for the sake of the wholeness of our child, as did Sarah's mom. The bottom line is that this letting go job is our responsibility. If we are expecting our child to lead us, then we are going to run into some troublesome snags in their separation process. Children *will* give us signs of their readiness, or not, for each new step of growing up. But *we* lead them to step with their confidence instead of their fear.

As our children grow out of childhood, letting go begins to gain dominance. We find ourselves doing more letting go and less holding on, although it will remain crucial for us to recognize the ways in which the holding on is still needed. Beginning in the late teen years and on into young adulthood, our letting go includes a gradual shift out of the role of parent and into a relationship of equals. We endeavor to show respect for and support of children's emerging adulthood. And with that final transition our actual letting go is complete. The parental love we feel for our child and the enduring urge to shelter him or her must be tempered by the knowledge that a deeper release is possible. It is possible to not only relinquish the parental role but also release our child from our emotional attachment.

119

No strings attached means our child is really free to create his own life separate from us.

Letting go of our adult children is as powerful and influential an act as our holding on to them in infancy. Generally a parent's failure to let go is the result of ignorance or fear. We don't notice when we should be letting go, or if we do notice we don't know how, or we are afraid. My fear of letting go was a result of not trusting that my child would be okay. I didn't know that he would adjust to age-appropriate challenges in his world, and that it was *good* for him to be allowed to do so. I didn't trust the wisdom of the growing up process for him.

Throughout childraising the balance of holding on and letting go is a juggling act of sorts. If we offer each aspect in proper measure, we will insure the healthy development of our children leading up to their final separation from us as they enter adulthood. If we have done our job well they will love us deeply and freely leave us behind.

AFTERWORD

In parenting, as in most endeavors, we will likely find that we are both good and bad at the job. Through the process of parenting our children, we generally win some measure of relief from the mistaken idea that we ought to be perfect. However, we all *do* have shortcomings, and unless we face and work with them, they'll run the show. If we don't acknowledge an aspect of ourselves that we'd rather not see, it has our blind spot to range freely within. Each of us faces this dilemma in ourselves.

The conscious parent has the powerful and potentially transformative tool of parenting-as-practice in her repertoire. The recipe for parenting-as-practice is equal parts contemplation and effort. Contemplation is whatever allows us to take stock of our life, mentally, physically and bodily. Contemplation traditionally takes the form of prayer and meditation. Effort is what is required to break through our unconsciouness in order to make positive change. *Life* is the arena of our efforting. We may study, exercise, or engage spiritual psychotherapy as part of our

effort. Contemplation and effort are intertwined, insepa-
rable. We can't have one without the other if we are looking to acquire a "whole new outlook."

The demand, discomfort, and joy of childraising is for
the benefit of our children – true – but it's for us too. We
hope to give our children the opportunity for a start in life
that we may not have had. They offer us the opportunity
to complete our own growth and maturation. Although it
may look like we are doing all the giving and making all
the sacrifices, in the end, we are the benefactors of what we
build in ourselves by reaching beyond our limits to love
them. That's the sacred task of parenting.

RECOMMENDED READING

Berends, Polly Berrien. (1997). *Whole Child/Whole Parent.* New York: HarperCollins.

Caplan, Mariana. (2002). *To Touch is To Live: The Need for Genuine Affection in an Impersonal World.* Prescott, Ariz.: Hohm Press.

Liedloff, Jean. (1986). *The Continuum Concept.* Reading, Mass.: Perseus Press.

Lozowick, Lee. (1997). *Conscious Parenting.* Prescott, Ariz.: Hohm Press.

Miller, Alice. (1981). *The Drama of the Gifted Child.* New York: Basic Books.

Pearce, Joseph Chilton. (1985). *Magical Child Matures.* New York: Dutton.

Pearce, Joseph Chilton. (1977). *Magical Child: Rediscovering Nature's Plan for Our Children.* New York: Dutton.

Rosemond, John. (1989). *John Rosemond's Six Point Plan for Raising Happy, Healthy Children.* Kansas City: Andrews and McMeel.

Samalin, Nancy. (1991). *Love & Anger, The Parental Dilemma.* New York: Viking Penguin.

Sandoz, Bobbie. (1993). *Parachutes for Parents:12 New Keys to Raising Children for a Better World.* Chicago: Contemporary Books.

Sears, William, M.D., and Martha Sears. (2001). *The Attachment Parenting Book : A Commonsense Guide to Understanding and Nurturing Your Baby.* New York: Little Brown and Company.

Thevenin, Tine. (1987). *The Family Bed.* New York: Perigee Books.

Thomas, Lalitha. (1997). *Ten Essential Foods.* Prescott, Ariz.: Hohm Press.

INDEX

A

acceptance, 64,70. *See also* love
    and acceptance
  self-, xii-xiii, xiv, xxii, 69-70,
    109, 111
action, wise/dispassionate, xvi-
    xvii, 11, 29, 81
advocating for children, 94-95
affection. *See* touch
aggression
  towards babies, 15
  boys, 20-21, 23
anger and resentment, 83, 110-
    111. *See also* sharp edges
archetypal mother and father,
    xix, xxi, 8
attachment-style parenting. *See*
    parenting, attachment-style
attention, xxii-xxiii, 12-24
  "attender," 18
  diffuse/focused, 17-18
  prioritizing, 13-14, 87-88
  undue, 7, 99-100, 101
  unwelcome, 15, 54

B

babies. *See* infants *and* infancy
backtracking work, xii.
"bardo," 82-83
basics, xxii-xxiii
"basic goodness," 5-6
"be-all and end-all," 67-68
birth order. *See* children, first
blueprint (biological), 4-5, 6, 7,
    19, 38
bottle-feeding, 39,40
boundaries, xxii-xxiii, 25-37
  as training, 28
  confusion over, 27-28
breast-feeding. *See* nursing
boys, 20-21
  vitality of, 23
  and girls, 20

C

chaos, dealing with, 87-88,
    105-106

125

sharing toys, 97-98
sharp edges, 107-109. *See also*
    anger and resentment
SIDS (Sudden Infant Death
    Syndrome), 55
sitting. *See* meditation
Sogyal Rinpoche, 82-83
spiritual
    community. *See* "tribe"
    practice, xiii, xiv, 29. *See also*
        parenting-as-practice
    teacher, xiv, xv, 81, 85
    teachings, xv, 81, 85. *See also*
        wisdom teachings
Steinitz, Purna, xv
sympathetic ear, 69-70

T

"tell me a story," 91-92
teen years, 44, 99, 101
Ten Essential Foods (Thomas),
    44
Thomas, Lalitha, 44
*The Tibetan Book of Living and
    Dying* (Sogyal Rinpoche),
    82-83
toddlers, 15-18, 97-98, 117
    and mealtimes. *See*
    children, mealtime with
    courage of, 17
    containing, 15-16
touch, xxii-xxiii, 52-64
training, acting against, xiii. *See
    also* parent, training of
transformation, xxii
"tribe," 1-2
Trungpa Rinpoche, Chögyam,
    5-6

U

unconscious habits (and
    beliefs), 46. *See also* parent-
    ing, program

V

village, "It takes a ___" (to raise
    a child), 65-66, 67

W

weaning, 42
welcoming a child, 6-8
"whole new outlook," xv, 122
wisdom teachings
    help of, 80-85
    modeling, 84-85
    parenting truths of, 84
work, 8-9, 34-37
    modeling, 35
"workbook," xv-xvi